Stop Sabotaging Your Confidence

How to transform self-sabotage into lasting
confidence and success

Dr Vesna Grubacevic, PhD

Keep shining &
inspiring!
Warmest wishes,
Dr. Vesna

First published in 2014 by Vesna Corporation Pty Ltd
Level 27, 101 Collins Street, Melbourne, Australia

Set in Linux Libertine

National Library of Australia Cataloguing-in-Publication entry:

Author:	Grubacevic, Vesna, author.
Title:	Stop sabotaging your confidence: how to transform self-sabotage into lasting confidence and success / Dr. Vesna Grubacevic; illustrations by Jane Pitkethly and David Blumenstein; photography by John Weninger.
ISBN:	9780992491307 (paperback)
Subjects:	Self-confidence.
	Self-actualization (Psychology).
	Success.
Other Authors/ Contributors:	Pitkethly, Jane, illustrator. Blumenstein, David, illustrator. Weninger, John, photographer.

Proofreading and production by Hourigan & Co.: hourigan.co

Illustrations in Chapters 1, 2, and 10 by Jane Pitkethly. Illustration in Chapter 6 by David Blumenstein. Author photo by John Weninger, Top Shots (topshots.com.au). Cover design by Design for Writers (designforwriters.com).

Find the author online: www.qttransformation.com

Contents

Dedication

This book is dedicated to you, the reader, for having the curiosity and courage to access your magnificent potential, and to increase your confidence and success.

To my gorgeous mother, Nevenka, whose ongoing loving support, encouragement and incredible commitment is reflected in this book.

To my amazing clients, for their commitment to themselves and their inspiration to others as to what is possible.

To my family, friends, colleagues, mentors, and everyone I have met along my journey. I am grateful for your support and for the lessons you have taught me and how this has shaped me along the way.

Thank you—you have helped me to help others so that together we can create an empowered society!

Preface

Many years ago I came across a quote that to this day inspires me to help people access their potential. Thomas Edison, the well-known inventor, said, "If we did all the things we are capable of doing we would truly astound ourselves."

Human beings are capable of so much more, yet we can underestimate ourselves and our ability. What causes us to limit ourselves, our confidence, and our success? How do so many people sabotage themselves and struggle to succeed while others excel and achieve incredible feats?

If you have ever wondered why you

- beat up on yourself or put yourself down,
- miss out on promotions or are not progressing in your career,
- are not making enough money or hesitate asking for a pay rise,
- settle for less than what you deserve in your career, relationships, and life,
- worry about your job security or about money,
- want everything to be perfect,
- let your family, friends, partner, colleagues, and manager treat you like a doormat,
- procrastinate about taking action, or
- lack clarity, passion, or direction in your life,

the exercises and techniques in this book will help you to discover how you are sabotaging your confidence and your success, and how you can end those patterns.

This book was born out of decades of my research, experience working with thousands of clients, and my own personal transformation. A theme that emerged over that time was self-sabotage—many clients came to see me to improve their self-confidence and to stop sabotaging themselves. Some were seeking help with improving their confidence in making decisions, others with improving their confidence in relationships, health, or finances, and still others sought to increase their confidence around public speaking and professional success.

These clients' lack of confidence led them to sabotage themselves. Each time I helped a client to stop the sabotage, their confidence and success increased significantly. I also noticed that most people have had confidence at one time or another in their lives, then "lost" it. Each time I helped a client to rediscover the confidence they once had, they also stopped sabotaging themselves and increased their success.

The principles in this book are based on models and research from varied disciplines, including NLP (neuro-linguistic programming), hypnosis, Q's behavioural change techniques, psychology, linguistics, and various branches of science (including physics, biology, neuroscience, and medicine).

This book is written for the layperson in a way which is easy to read, understand, apply, and integrate into daily life. To this end, detailed references have been left out of this book; they are available on request.

The main techniques in this book draw on three key disciplines: NLP, hypnosis, and Q's behavioural change techniques. They will help you reprogram your thoughts, feelings, and behaviours to build strong levels of confidence and to develop a mindset of success.

NLP is a powerful set of techniques for maximising human potential and performance. It enables us to understand how we think and communicate, and how we produce behaviours and results. NLP is all about the "how"—the process of human behaviour. By understanding the process of how we think, feel, and act, we can change the process and therefore, our behaviour, our confidence, and our success.

Because NLP works with the unconscious, the change in behaviour is very fast. Rather than taking twenty-one days or more to change a behaviour or habit, with NLP the change can take effect within hours or even minutes (depending on the behaviour, the client's willingness to change, and the change being made).

NLP assists with two main areas:

1. changing unwanted behaviours and patterns
2. improving communication and personal and professional relationships

Hypnosis is a related discipline. It is simply learning how to go into a relaxed state, which we call a trance. What is interesting about this is that we put ourselves into a trance every day. When was the last time you were watching a movie and you were so involved in it you lost track of time and were unaware of any distractions around you – you were totally involved in only the movie? You were in a movie trance. Or perhaps the last time you drove your car, you drove half way to your destination and then suddenly realised where you were, and wondered how you arrived there. You were in a driving trance.

In all those instances, you were fully awake and relaxed.

So trance is a natural, normal waking state that we go into any time our attention is totally focused on one thing. Because only we can control our thoughts, feelings and actions, when we are in trance only we are in control. The hypnotherapist simply assists us to enter a relaxed state of trance so that we can communicate more effectively with our own unconscious. Entering trance allows us to stop the analytical brain—the internal chatter—so that we can communicate directly with the unconscious to create the changes we desire in our lives.

Q^t's behavioural change techniques are new, developed by me through my PhD research and further studies. They incorporate NLP, hypnosis, and several of the other disciplines mentioned earlier, to assist you to more effectively respond to and deal with people's behaviour.

On a personal note, I have had many challenges with lack of confidence in my life, both personally and professionally. I will draw on my personal transformation journey (growing from decades of being bullied to becoming a confident and successful business owner), and my experiences to assist you on your journey. Because the focus of this book is YOU and your journey, rather than sharing my life journey with you, I have emphasised self-awareness and empowerment through the information and exercises in this book.

This is a self-empowerment book. It aims to empower you with simple, easy to understand and apply exercises and techniques, which you can instantly use to discover the confidence and success that lies within you right now. While there are hundreds of different techniques that I could share with you, because I want to keep this book easy to use and the techniques easy to implement, I have selected several dozen techniques which will empower you to quickly improve your confidence and success.

It is important that you complete these exercises and use the suggested techniques so that you receive more value and benefits from reading this book. As you work through this book, each chapter will also offer you insights and learnings to help you to easily design and implement your own practice plan.

This book is divided into three phases, to reflect three phases of the reader's journey:

Phase 1: "Your Confidence Saboteurs," which will assist you to become aware of and to identify how you may be sabotaging yourself, your confidence, and your success right now.

Phase 2: "Transform Your Confidence," where you will learn practical techniques to empower yourself to begin changing your thoughts, feelings, and behaviours for greater confidence and success.

Phase 3: "Your Practice Plan," where you will be guided through designing your own practice plan so you can integrate the tools in this book into your daily life and success.

I encourage you to also email me with any questions, and to share your insights and successes with me.

You can reach me at vesna@qttransformation.com.

Congratulations on making a commitment to yourself and to your success. Reading this book and completing the exercises in it are the first steps to your transformation. Enjoy your journey. I look forward to empowering you.

Phase I

Your confidence saboteurs

1. Stop hypnotising yourself to fail

How to stop excusing yourself from success

Human potential, though not always apparent, is there waiting to be discovered and invited forth.

—William W. Purkey, Author, Professor Emeritus, University of North Carolina

1.1   Self-talk

Do you realise that every time you talk to yourself you are hypnotising yourself? As you listen to your internal dialogue, pay attention to whether it is positive or negative. Are you hypnotising yourself with negative self-talk by putting yourself down or judging or criticising yourself, or with positive self-talk by speaking to yourself with love, acknowledgement, and kindness?

Every time you speak, every thought you have, each emotion you feel, you are either programming yourself for success or failure. This is because these words and thoughts act as direct suggestions to your mind. Every thought you have affects how you feel, which in turn affects your behaviour. For example, when you are thinking that an activity will be difficult, you probably feel worried about getting it done, and as a result, you put off doing it. In contrast, when you are thinking and expecting that an activity will be fun and easy, you probably feel motivated to do it and you do it with ease.

We are hypnotising ourselves daily with our self-talk. Your self-talk is self-hypnosis. You are putting yourself into a negative hypnotic trance when your words, thoughts, and emotions are negative, and into a positive hypnotic trance when your words, thoughts, and emotions are positive.

For most people, if their thoughts, words, and emotions are negative, generally they are hypnotising themselves to fail and are negatively affecting their confidence. In contrast, if their thoughts, words, and emotions are positive, generally they are hypnotising themselves to succeed and boosting their confidence.

Infinite potential

From an NLP point of view, everyone has all the resources they need to succeed—we have infinite potential to achieve success. You only need to read the Guinness World Records books to see the incredible feats that humans have achieved. The 2013 edition of the Guinness World Records makes the observation that humans have the drive to overcome obstacles and psychological and physical barriers. While it took 190,000 years of evolution for a human to run a mile in less than four minutes, at least 366 people have broken that record since.

Human beings have unrealised potential within them. Have you ever done something and surprised yourself as to how easy or quick it was? Perhaps you went to a job interview and it went better than you expected. Or perhaps you felt more at ease than you thought you would on a first date. Generally, we tend to underestimate our potential until we push ourselves beyond our comfort zone and realise how much more we are capable of achieving.

You are capable of so much more; you just need to learn to access the infinite resources within you more effectively. I believe that the only thing that differentiates a highly confident and successful person from one that is less confident and successful is how each of them accesses their internal resources. How you tap into your infinite potential is governed by your thought processes (including whether your self-talk is positive or negative), emotions, and behaviours, as we will explore in this book.

1.2   Confidence and success

What is confidence?

Confidence is a positive emotion that reflects your level of self-belief and self-worth. The greater your belief in yourself and your worth, the greater your level of confidence in yourself and your abilities.

Confidence versus competence

Sometimes we can confuse confidence with competence. Confidence is an emotion, while competence relates to our level of skill and ability. Both confidence and competence are important for success in life. One without the other may compromise our level of success.

For example, a manager may have great competence or skills in their industry, yet their lack of confidence may prevent them from making calls, from delegating effectively, from speaking in front of large groups, and so on. Alternatively, a manager who has enormous confidence and meets lots of people, yet lacks the competence to turn those opportunities into business, may spend far too much time in unproductive meetings or may not have the communication skills to effectively deal with challenging people.

Both confidence and competence are important keys to success. You probably know of people who have lots of confidence yet fail to deliver results, lack substance in what they say, and talk themselves up without delivering on their promises. You may also know of people who have lots of skills, yet their lack of confidence prevents them from sharing their ideas and skills with others; they find it difficult to promote themselves effectively and may even question their contribution.

Imagine that you would like more confidence to speak in public: you will need to address any fears, self-doubts, and limiting beliefs that are affecting your levels of confidence. In order for you to increase your competence, you will need to learn some communication skills around public speaking. Both are important for confidence, as greater competence increases confidence further, and greater confidence helps people to learn new skills. Competence builds confidence. Confidence helps you to practise skills to build your competence, which in turn builds your confidence. I call this the confidence–competence cycle (figure 1.1).

With both confidence and competence, you can achieve the personal and professional success you desire. First, in Chapters 1–7 of this book, we will focus on empowering you to increase your confidence. Then we will assist you to develop your

Confidence–competence cycle

Figure 1.1: The confidence–competence cycle

competence (in particular, your skills around communication and relating to people personally and professionally) in Chapters 8 and 9. Finally, Chapter 10 will help you to integrate the techniques and learnings in this book, and practice your new skills for ongoing confidence and success.

Feedback for success

An important belief in NLP is that there is only feedback, never failure. This means that your level of confidence and success in your relationship, career/business, health, finances, family, friends, personal growth, and all areas of life, is your feedback to you as to how you are doing in those areas. This also provides you with feedback as to what you need to change to improve your confidence and your success.

For example, if in your career you keep missing out on promotions or a pay increase, it is simply feedback to you to change what you are now doing so you can succeed. Do you need to:

- improve your confidence in yourself?
- improve your performance at work?
- improve your people or communication skills?
- improve your ability to promote yourself, your ideas, and your skills?
- change any beliefs that are holding you back so that you can ask for a promotion or pay increase, and sound confident and believable as you ask for it?
- change your career so that you are more passionate about what you are doing?
- change or improve something else?
- change or improve a combination of the above?

It is important that if what you are now doing is not helping you to achieve the success you desire, to use that as feedback to change your approach and to do something different to succeed. Instead of beating up on yourself for your lack of success or thinking that you have failed, use the lack of success as feedback to help you to learn and improve.

Confidence and context

Are there some areas of life in which you feel confident and others in which you lack confidence? While it is possible to lack confidence at all times, most people have confidence in some areas of life and lack it in others. There may be different contexts (areas of life) in which confidence may be present for you, lacking entirely, or be there somewhat.

Let's take stock of where you are now in each area of your life, and the level of confidence and success you have right now. For example, a person may say that in their family they have a 4 out of 10 level of confidence and have a 3 out of 10 level of success. What they need to improve is to stop feeling not good enough when family members put down their achievements.

Rate your current level of confidence and success out of 10 (10 being high) for each area of your life. Next to each one, note the things you need to improve or change to increase your scores. Write your scores and comments in the table below. Feel free to change the areas of life to suit you. A couple of blank spaces have been included in the table below for you to add in any additional areas that are important in your life right now.

Area of life	Level of confidence	Level of success	Things to improve/change to increase my scores
Career/business			
Relationship			
Family			
Friends			
Finances			
Health			
Self-development			

Area of life	Level of confidence	Level of success	Things to improve/change to increase my scores
Hobbies			

As you look at the scores, remember it is your feedback as to how well you are doing in each area of your life at the moment. It is also your feedback as to what you can improve or change to increase the above scores, and therefore, your confidence and success in those areas. The rest of this book will assist you with this.

What affects your confidence and your success?

Your level of confidence and success can vary in different contexts. What affects your confidence and success in each context is determined by a range of influences, including your family upbringing, religious and cultural values and beliefs, peers and friends, education, media and the internet, and past experiences.

Family upbringing

For example, how did your parents interact with each other, with you, and your siblings when you were growing up? Did they encourage high self-esteem and confidence, or did they frown upon it as "being too big for your boots" or "being big-headed"?

Religious and cultural values and beliefs

Some cultures and religions have beliefs and social expectations that can be limiting. For example, there may be the belief that people need to be punished for having too much money, a need to feel guilty for having more than other people, and so on. Meanwhile, other cultural and religious values and beliefs encourage confidence and success.

Peers and friends

Was there peer pressure from friends to behave in certain ways so you belonged in the "cool" group and felt confident and successful? For example, was smoking or drinking the accepted way to be confident and more successful? Or was being "good" and "smart" the accepted way to feel confident and successful among your peers?

Education

Was the education you received in school empowering? Did it encourage you to have confidence in your ability to learn and succeed in school and in life? Or was learning and study a traumatic or negative experience which reduced your levels of confidence and success?

Media and the internet

What are the values and beliefs predominant in the TV shows and movies you watch, the books you read, the radio stations you listen to, and the online activities you enjoy? To what extent do they influence your behaviour, confidence, and success?

Past experiences

The meaning we give to our past experiences will define those past experiences as either good or bad, a success or a failure, pleasant or unpleasant, boring or fun, and so on. It is not the experiences themselves that are, for example, fun or boring; they are simply past events. It is how we **interpret** those events and experiences that define our meanings of them.

Were your past experiences of being confident and successful pleasant or unpleasant? How were you treated by your partner, family, friends, colleagues, and manager when you felt confident and successful at an activity? How much did they support you? Are you expecting your future experiences to be the same or different?

All of the above influences can combine to form our current values, beliefs, thoughts, emotions, and behaviours around confidence and success. For some people, the above can culminate in high levels of confidence and empowering beliefs around confidence and success. For others it can result in negative emotions (e.g. fear, hurt, anger, resentment) and disempowering beliefs around being confident and successful (e.g. "I am not worthy of success," "I am not good enough," or "if I have success I will need to be punished").

Importantly, we never judge whether the above influences are good or bad, right or wrong. We simply look at them for the purpose of understanding how they affect our current levels of confidence and success. Then, if these influences are affecting your confidence and success negatively, we can assist you to change them. We will cover how to do that in the subsequent chapters of this book.

1.3   *Responsibility*

It is important for you to take responsibility for your confidence and success. Equally important is for you to take responsibility for your lack of confidence or lack of success, rather than blame other people, your circumstances, or yourself for not having the confidence and success you desire.

People who take responsibility for their own life are far more successful than those that make excuses for not having what they want. Taking responsibility empowers you to have the confidence and success you desire. Making excuses or blaming others, your circumstances or yourself disempowers you and sabotages your confidence and success.

> **Responsibility Increases Confidence and Success**
>
> **Excuses/Blame Sabotage Confidence and Success**

There are potentially many excuses. Some common ones include:

- the weather, e.g. it is too cold or hot for exercise
- the traffic, e.g. being late because of traffic
- the economy, e.g. sales are up or down because of the economy
- other people, e.g. she hurt me, he makes me mad
- the organisation, e.g. the bureaucracy and red tape
- money, e.g. not enough, too expensive
- time, e.g. not enough, too busy
- upbringing, e.g. not having opportunities, negative family environment

Excuses are reflected in the language and the self-talk that we use. When you hear "yes, we can, but..." usually an excuse follows the "but." When you hear "I can't... It won't..." and so on, these are also excuses. Underpinning these excuses are often unconscious beliefs that sabotage your success. For example, if someone consistently makes the excuse "I can't afford it" (whether via their self-talk or spoken language) after a while that becomes their reality. Their whole life revolves around lack and that is what they keep creating for as long as they have that belief. They program their mind for lack and scarcity, and miss seeing opportunities as they present themselves. They hypnotise themselves with that negative self-talk and language that then affects their behaviour negatively. We will discuss the significance of beliefs in Chapter 4.

Any time you hear anyone rationalise why they do not have the success that they want, they are making excuses for not having their success. For example, "I did not reach my sales target this month because of the economy." What is interesting is that in the same economic environment, I have heard salespeople say, "My sales are up this month because of the economy." Consider an alternative example: "Because of my upbringing, I did not have the same opportunities as others; that is why I am not successful now." Other people with similar upbringings go out and create amazing opportunities for themselves and stop their upbringing from being an excuse for their lack of success.

Excuses are just that—reasons for not having the success that we want. Excuses stop us from achieving our full potential. Once we stop making excuses, our confidence and success improve dramatically.

Blame is an excuse

Any time you blame someone or something else for why you do not have the success you desire, you are excusing yourself from success. Even blaming yourself or beating up on yourself is a good way to excuse yourself from success. Dwelling on what you should have done or why you didn't do something is a good way to stay stuck in the past rather than moving on with your life.

Sometimes you may be aware of the excuses you are making (e.g. saying or thinking "I was late because of traffic"). Other times you may be unaware of your excuses because they are unconscious beliefs that limit you (e.g. "I am not worthy of success"). When I refer to the traffic example as an excuse, some say it isn't, because they correctly point out that you can't change traffic. Let me explain what I mean.

There are three things that you can personally control: how you think, how you feel, and how you act or react to people and to situations. You can also influence others through your communication. Everything and everyone else is outside of your control, including traffic. What is within your control is:

- How you feel about going to your destination. Are you looking forward to it or dreading it?
- How you are thinking about where you are going. Will you be on time or late? Will the event be successful or unsuccessful?
- How you are behaving. Do you leave on time, early, or late? Do you take the quick or long way to get there? Do you leave it to the last minute to get prepared, then leave flustered?

All of this will affect how you relate to traffic. If you left late or under pressure, time seems to never be enough. If you left on time, you feel relaxed and time is abundant. The state you are in (i.e. how you are feeling) in traffic will be how you interpret time. According to quantum physics, time and space are not absolute; they are relative to a particular observer. You have probably noticed how "time flies when you are having fun" and how time drags on when you are disinterested in what is happening around you. So while you are unable to control traffic, you can control how you feel, think, and act before, during, and after being in traffic.

Likewise, any time you overreact with emotions to what other people say or do (e.g. go into a road rage or a jealous rage), you are the one feeling the emotions. The other person is simply being themselves—how you react to them is your re-sponsibility. If your "buttons" are being pushed and you take other people's comments or actions too personally, that is your responsibility because you are the one thinking, feeling, and acting that way towards them. Likewise, if your "buttons" are pushed while reading and completing the exercises in this book, remember that they are your "buttons" and your responsibility to acknowledge and address.

By blaming others for how you feel, you are giving away your control over yourself and effectively saying that they are controlling you. Please remember that how you think, feel, and act is your sole responsibility. If you choose to give away that responsibility by blaming others, you are giving away your responsibility to change how you think, feel, and act, and preventing yourself from being even more confident and successful. The most successful people in life take total responsibility for, and are masters of, their own thoughts, feelings, and actions.

Decisions and responsibility

With decision comes great responsibility. If you don't make a decision, then you need not do anything about it. Once you make a decision, then you need to do something about it; you need to be responsible for that decision and act on it.

What decisions have you not made that are holding you back from being more confident and successful? For example, have you yet to make decisions about a job, a promotion, a relationship, finances, starting a business, pursuing a dream, ending dysfunctional personal or professional relationships, or stopping unwanted habits? Make a note of these below.

Congratulations, you have just made a decision—you have decided that you have yet to make the above decisions. Decision-making is easy. It is the action required to follow through on decisions that holds most people back from making them. Their fears, self-doubts, and limiting beliefs prevent them from making decisions. For example, some people fear rejection, and so stop themselves from applying for a promotion or making their next career move. We will discuss these limiting factors in detail, and you will be able to explore your own saboteurs in the next chapter of this book.

How are you excusing yourself from success?

Now consider each area of your life again. This time, honestly think about and write in the table below what is now preventing you from having greater confidence and success in each of those areas of life. What excuses are you making? Who or what are you blaming for your situation? For example, some things that may be preventing a person from having success in their health could be: beliefs (I can't lose weight, fear of failure), emotional eating, saying it is too hard, or not wanting to make a lifestyle change. Again, you can change the areas of life in the table below to suit you, as well as adding in extra areas of life as appropriate.

Area of life	What is now preventing you from having greater confidence and success? What excuses are you making? Who or what are you blaming for your situation?
Career/business	
Relationship	

Area of life	What is now preventing you from having greater confidence and success? What excuses are you making? Who or what are you blaming for your situation?
Family	
Friends	
Finances	
Health	
Self-development	
Hobbies	

Notice the excuses you are making and who you are blaming in each of those areas of life. Make a note of the themes you notice below.

_____

_____

_____

_____

_____

_____

_____

_____

_____

We will explore these excuses and how to change them in the rest of this book.

Control versus influence

Some people get angry or frustrated because they want to control things, situations, or people that are out of their control. For example, people get frustrated because their partner continues to be messy at home.

As mentioned earlier and summarised in the table below, you can only control yourself and how you think, feel and act or react to people and situations. In addition, you can influence other people through your communication. Other people are also in control of how they feel, think and act, and how they influence you.

You control *your*	Other people control *their*
Thoughts	Thoughts
Feelings	Feelings
Actions and reactions	Actions and reactions
Plus you can influence each other through your communication.	

When you focus on what other people are thinking or feeling, or what they do or don't do, that is when frustration and anger can occur. In turn, this can affect your level of confidence and success.

You can only control the meaning you give to situations and how you respond to other people and situations. Avoid getting frustrated or angry about the things that are out of your control. Instead, focus on what is within your control, i.e. how you respond with your thoughts, emotions, actions, and communication. Chapters 3–9 of this book will assist you with this.

Where is your focus?

Take a moment now to think about the past month and all the times you felt angry or frustrated. Note these in the table below. Next to each event or situation, write down whether you were focusing on your thoughts, your feelings, and your actions at the time, or on events or people beyond your control.

Event or situation	My focus
e.g. sitting in traffic	*e.g. other drivers going too slow*

Notice that if you had shifted your focus to you, you would have been in greater charge of those situations. For example, a more productive use of your time in traffic (instead of feeling frustrated by the traffic) could have been to think about your upcoming meeting, what you wanted to achieve, and feeling good about the meeting going well.

For each of the above events, write down how you would have preferred to think, feel, and act in each of those events, so that you would have felt more in charge in those situations.

Event or situation	My preferred focus
e.g. sitting in traffic	*e.g. thinking about my meeting being a success*

Next time you are in any of the above situations, remember to focus on yourself instead.

The responsibility paradox

Some people take insufficient responsibility for their success (or lack thereof) by blaming other people, situations, or themselves, and making excuses for not having the success they desire. Because they take insufficient responsibility and expect other people to help them or rely on things around them changing, they don't take sufficient action to achieve success. In turn, this lack of success can decrease their level of confidence.

Others take too much responsibility for other people's thoughts, feelings, and actions. If you take too much responsibility for people:

- you may disempower those people as they will never realise the consequences of their actions or inaction
- other people may continue to be irresponsible
- other people become too reliant on you and never achieve their potential
- you will disempower yourself by focusing on what you cannot control
- while your focus is on helping others too much, you may have less focus on looking after yourself and taking action to increase your own success

Taking too much responsibility for others limits you and them, and in the process your confidence and success, and theirs, may suffer.

When it comes to responsibility, you want to take just the right amount of responsibility for yourself by focusing on how you feel, think and act, and the right amount of responsibility for others by focusing on how you can influence and empower them through your communication. By taking too much responsibility for others, you disempower them and yourself. By taking too little responsibility for yourself, you disempower yourself. By taking no responsibility for how you influence others, you disempower them and yourself. It is very much the "Goldilocks" scenario—you neither want to take too much responsibility, nor too little. Instead, you want the amount to be just right!

When you take full responsibility for yourself, you stop excusing yourself from success and stop hypnotising yourself to fail. In the next chapter, we will discuss the different ways that people can sabotage their confidence and success, and you will also identify your own patterns of sabotage in the self-assessment quiz.

1.4 Summary

The key messages that we covered in this chapter include:

- You are hypnotising yourself daily with your self-talk and your excuses.
- Success is a combination of confidence and competence.
- People who take responsibility for their lives are more successful than those that make excuses or blame themselves, others, and their circumstances.
- You can personally control how you think, feel, and act and also how you influence others through your communication.
- You want to take the right amount of responsibility for yourself and others—not too much and not too little ... the amount that is just right!

1.5   *Your action journey*

What action will you now take after having read this chapter? Please note your action items from this chapter in your practice plan in Chapter 10 of this book.

2. The art of self-sabotage

How are you sabotaging yourself?

Man can learn nothing except by going from the known to the unknown.

—Claude Bernard, Physiologist

Would you like to discover how you are sabotaging your confidence and your success? In how many different ways do you undermine yourself? How, specifically, are you hindering your confidence and your success?

Sabotage occurs any time you want to achieve something and then your actions, or lack of action, prevent you from being, doing, or having what you want in life. Any time you undermine yourself and your success, or you hinder, prevent, or undo your work, you are sabotaging yourself either consciously or unconsciously.

Sabotage is an art. People who sabotage themselves are often very good at sabotaging their confidence and their success. They have unconsciously mastered how to sabotage themselves through years of repeating the same behaviour. Humans are creatures of habit, running the same behaviours and patterns, and staying in the comfort zone until they decide to make a change.

2.1   What drives our behaviour?

Before we discuss how you specifically may be sabotaging your confidence and your success, let us first understand what drives our behaviour and our level of confidence and success.

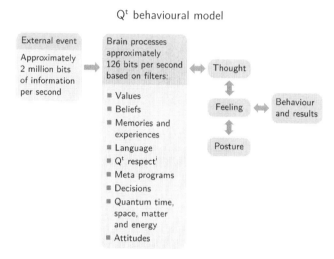

Figure 2.1: What drives our behaviour?

Figure 2.1 summarises how we perceive ourselves and other people, and how that perception affects our confidence, behaviour, and success. Because our thoughts affect how we feel and act, it is important to understand how to take charge of our thinking, so that we can take charge of our emotions, behaviour, and success. Best estimates by researchers show that every second around two million bits of information surround us. Our brain's capacity can only handle around 126 bits of information per second.

Mihaly Csikszentmihalyi estimates the amount of information

that the nervous system can process at any given time as about 126 bits of information per second. These bits are more than the "bits" referred to when we think of computers. Our nervous system selects the 126 bits of information that are relevant to us based on several filters (including our values, beliefs, and past memories).

Those filters determine our personality and how we interpret and perceive the people and situations around us; they define our model of the world. Because each person has a unique combination of filters, different things will be relevant to them at a point in time. Therefore, each person will take in different bits of information that they will use to interpret as their reality.

This is why two people can go through exactly the same experience and come out with very different interpretations of the situation. For example, your recollection of past family gatherings may be different to that of your siblings. You have probably watched a movie with a friend, and found that you liked the movie while your friend disliked it. You both watched the same movie, yet you each interpreted that movie different-ly.

The filters include the following, along with several others:

- **Values**. Our priorities and motivations; they define what is important to us e.g. family, money, success, work–life balance.
- **Beliefs**. Convictions about what is true for us. They are rules that we have around what we can do and what we believe is true about the world.
- **Memories and experiences**. Memories are based on our past experiences in life. We discussed past experiences in

reference to confidence and success in Chapter 1.

- **Language.** We acquire language at a specific age. We can also learn other languages that give us different perspectives on life.
- **Q^t respect[i].** A new filter and set of behavioural change techniques discovered by Dr Vesna Grubacevic, which relate to how you respond to and deal with people's behaviour.

Referring back to the above diagram, you will notice that as an external event is processed through the above filters, we create a thought of that event. For example, if we are offered a job interview by a potential new employer (the external event), we have a thought about that (e.g. thinking of securing that job).

Our thought is made up of any combination of the five senses: visual (pictures), auditory (sounds), kinaesthetic (feelings), olfactory (smells), and gustatory (tastes), plus auditory digital (our self-talk). For example, as we think about securing that job we may be imagining ourselves smiling when we hear the good news. Our thought is linked with a certain feeling (e.g. confidence, happiness, motivation, sadness) and with our posture (i.e. how we sit and stand). For example, we may be feeling excited about the interview and sitting upright in our chair as we think about it.

All of this (our thoughts, feelings, and posture) affects our behaviour, our level of success and results. By understanding how our thoughts, feelings, and behaviours affect our current level of confidence and success, we can become more aware and make the appropriate changes to achieve our desired level of confidence and success.

2.2   Our patterns become comfortable

We are unconsciously conditioning ourselves to respond to our environment with our thoughts, our emotions, and our behaviours. We condition ourselves to run the same patterns and to do the same behaviour. After a while, it becomes effortless: an automatic behaviour that we do unconsciously, without thinking about it. It is like driving a car. The first time we learn to drive a car, we are very conscious of everything. Remember your first driving lesson and how you were so conscious of the clutch, gears, rear-view mirror, and side mirrors? Now, you reach your destination safely without thinking about how to drive. You automatically know how to do it.

The more we run the same pattern of behaviour, the stronger that pattern becomes. Neuroscientists have shown that all information (including our memories) is stored in the connections between the synapses. The more we use a neural connection in our mind-body, the stronger it gets, while any neglected ones are deleted.

Our patterns of behaviour become comfortable for us. At the same time, it is important to adapt to changing environments, whether these be the changing economy or a personal or professional situation. If you stay in your comfortable patterns of behaviour, it makes it more difficult to adapt, to feel confident, and to succeed in a new environment.

The comfort zone

The comfort zone is so named because it is comfortable. We get used to living life in a certain way and, unless something dramatic happens to propel us out of the comfort zone, we continue doing what we are used to. Despite feeling unhappy or unfulfilled, we persist with the current lifestyle because it is all we know, and to step out of what we know can be scary.

Some people are successful yet they are still unfulfilled, because they know deep down inside that there is more that they can achieve; they thirst for more. Again, to venture out of something that they know, where they are successful anyway, is uncomfortable. Regardless of whether you are highly confident and successful or not, after a while, wherever you are in life, it becomes your comfort zone.

I call the comfort zone the "stale" zone. People who are in the comfort zone for too long get "stale," feel bored or frustrated, and are unfulfilled.

The 'growth' zone lies outside our comfort zone

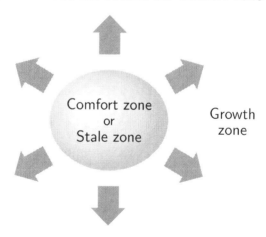

Figure 2.2: The growth zone

The only way to learn and to grow as people is to step out of the "stale" zone and to challenge ourselves. Most new learning can only happen in the "growth" zone, which lies outside our comfort zone (see Figure 2.2).

The laws of physics apply to everything in the universe; humans operate by the same laws. According to Galileo's Law of Inertia, motion itself requires no force. Motion can continue without any force. It is only changes in motion that require pushes and pulls. For example, a ball will continue rolling along a flat surface with the same speed and in the same direction until something or someone does something to alter its speed or direction. A child kicking the ball or the wind blowing the ball in another direction are examples of pushes and pulls. Likewise, human behaviour has a natural state of motion. It is only pushes and pulls by you, other people, situations, and your environment that can lead people to make a change and to step out of their comfort zone. Without those pushes and pulls, people stay in their comfort zone.

Trapped in a comfort zone

Often we can be trapped in our comfort zone. There are several ways that you can identify that you may be in your comfort zone:

- life feels like a "rat race," a treadmill, "same old"
- you have dreams, and your fears and self-doubts prevent you from taking action towards them
- you put off doing the things you really want to do to achieve your goals
- you lack direction, purpose, and goals in your career, relationship, or life

- you feel frustrated and unfulfilled with your career, relationship, health, finances, and life, yet you do nothing about it
- you shy away from taking any risks and crave the security of what you now know
- you have stagnated at work and in your relationships—things have become mundane, unexciting, or boring
- you lack challenge and growth and find everything you do too easy and automatic
- you gravitate towards the familiar (e.g. same restaurant, same holiday destinations, same job, same route to work, same weekend activities) rather than seeking out new adventures and experiences.

Known versus unknown

Being creatures of habit, we can allow ourselves to be trapped by our comfort zone. Often we opt for the easy way, for mediocrity, for what we know because what we don't know is unknown—it is unfamiliar. The comfort zone keeps us trapped because we mistakenly believe that the "known" is safe.

Often the "known" can be unsafe and disempowering if our thoughts, emotions and behaviours limit us. When the "known" disempowers us or has us stay in dysfunctional personal or professional relationships, the "known" becomes the uncomfortable zone. Yet some people stay there and remain unhappy because of their fears and self-doubts. For example, someone who believes that they are undeserving of happiness will put up with dysfunctional personal and professional relationships because they believe that they do not deserve any better.

Once the past fears and self-doubts are addressed, they stop recreating the same past dysfunctional relationships and situations. Then, the "unknown" future becomes much safer. You feel empowered and confident to attract and create the future you desire—the scary and uncertain "unknown" is transformed into a certain, safe and fulfilling new "known." The rest of this book will empower you to transform the "unknown" into a new fulfilling "known."

Confidence busters

From a physics perspective, because it takes no force to keep something moving, the real question is, how did it begin to move in the first place? Similarly, it takes no force or effort to keep a pattern of sabotage recurring—it has a natural momentum. It is an unconscious pattern that we automatically run, which is often out of our conscious awareness. The real question then is, how did the sabotage begin and what triggered it?

Most people have had confidence at one time or another in their life, then "lost" it. Hence the question you need to answer is—when did you sabotage your confidence? Events happen in our lives that we interpret in a way that reduces our confidence. Common types of events, or confidence busters as I call them, include the following:

At work/in business

- failed projects, missing out on a promotion or a series of sales or deals
- being moved sideways, demoted, or performance managed

- receiving a poor performance assessment
- being retrenched or fired from a job, or job relocation
- being promoted or being given a challenging project, feeling out of our depth, and questioning our ability to succeed at it
- being harshly criticised by other people; being ignored, isolated, teased, harassed, or bullied
- conflict in or failed business partnerships, loss of good staff or customers
- business growing too fast and being unable to manage growth effectively

In relationships

- getting engaged or married and questioning our decision or our ability as a partner
- giving birth to or adopting a child and questioning our parenting ability
- difficulty conceiving or giving birth, loss of a baby
- separation, divorce, or break-up from a partner
- staying in an abusive or dysfunctional personal relationship

With family and friends

- new additions to the family (e.g. sibling, niece or nephew, grandchild) and questioning ourselves
- conflict in a family: with parents, siblings, other relatives, in-laws, ex-partners, stepchildren, step-parents
- loss of a friendship or difficulty forming new friendships
- children moving out of home or moving back home
- new friends and questioning whether we will fit in or be

accepted
- too much pressure from peers, parents, teachers, or ourselves to perform
- learning difficulties, poor marks, or failed subjects at school
- moving overseas, to another city, or from city to country or vice versa

In finances

- receiving a financial windfall and not being sure how to manage it
- a financial loss, bankruptcy, or being sued
- high debt levels
- low levels of savings or income
- loss of a major customer or deal

In health

- being overweight, putting on weight, or poor body image
- illness or injury affecting our mobility or energy levels
- illness or injury affecting a loved one's mobility or well-being
- death of a close family member or friend
- emotional or mental health challenges (e.g. addictions to unhealthy substances, depression, phobias, fears and anxieties, emotional breakdown, other mental health issues)

These can all be confidence busters, as can any other event that pushes us out of our comfort zone so we find it difficult to cope or we question ourselves. As a result, our confidence can be negatively affected.

As you look at the above list of events, ask—do any apply to you? If so, how did each of those events contribute to your "loss" of confidence and affect your success?

2.3   *How do you sabotage yourself?*

Let us now turn to the different ways that you can sabotage yourself, your confidence, and your success. While there are many ways that people can sabotage their confidence and success, below is a summary of the most common patterns of sabotage that I have encountered from working with thousands of clients. You may be aware of some of these patterns consciously and others may be unconscious patterns for you. To assist you, these patterns have been placed in general categories. Some of these patterns may overlap across more than one category, depending on how you run the sabotage patterns. All of these patterns will be further discussed in the following chapters of this book. Feel free to add in any others that apply to you in the table below.

Your language

1. **Excuses.** In Chapter 1 we already discussed excuses and how you may be excusing yourself from success. Most excuses result from limiting beliefs.
2. **Blame.** We also discussed blame and not taking enough responsibility in Chapter 1. To the extent that you blame other people, yourself, or your upbringing for your current situation in life, you are keeping yourself stuck where you are now.

3. **Beating up on yourself/negative self talk.** Do you put yourself down, talk down to yourself, or beat up on yourself? How you speak about yourself to others and to yourself has a significant impact on your confidence and on your success.

4. **Putting other people down.** When you criticise, are overly judgemental, gossip about other people, or put other people down, you are focusing on others and taking your focus off yourself. This in turn affects your confidence and your success.

5. **Disempowering language.** Do you use words that limit you (e.g. can't, should, have to) or those that empower you (e.g. can, want to, will)? The words we speak often reflect our beliefs.

Your thoughts

6. **Self-doubts.** Do you overanalyse, second-guess, or question yourself, or doubt yourself and your abilities? Feeling insecure in yourself and having low self-belief results in low confidence or lack of confidence, and undermines your success.

7. **Limiting beliefs.** Beliefs (such as fear of failure, fear of success, fear of rejection, fear of public speaking, "I am not good enough," "I can't have what I want") limit your confidence and your success.

8. **Internal conflicts.** Are you sending mixed signals to other people? Do you feel confused about what to do in life? Internal conflicts pull us in different directions, dilute our focus, and affect our confidence and success as a result.

9. **Lack of clarity, direction, and goals.** Do you lack passion or a clear direction for your life? Not knowing what you really want leads to scattered thinking and results in scattered action. We will assist you with developing your clarity, confidence, and success throughout this book.

10. **Comparing yourself to others.** If you compare yourself to others too much it can affect your self-image, self-esteem, confidence and success. These comparisons are often based on negative emotions and limiting beliefs.

11. **Lack of clear priorities.** Do you find it difficult to prioritise tasks? Without priorities, we can be overwhelmed, as everything takes on the same importance or urgency.

12. **Feeling unloved.** Are you hurt when your partner or family don't show you enough love or attention? Is your neediness for love pushing people away? Feelings of being unloved can affect our levels of confidence and success.

13. **Feeling intimidated by other people.** Do you feel threatened or intimidated by other people or situations? Do you feel jealous when other people succeed? These may negatively affect your confidence to do things, and hence affect your success.

14. **Feeling stuck or trapped.** Do you feel stagnated, unfulfilled, or bored? Do you stay in relationships or jobs in which you are unhappy? We already discussed how we can be trapped in a comfort zone and how this can compromise our confidence and success.

15. **Not trusting other people.** Do you fear being hurt, and so protect yourself from other people? Does your lack

of trust prevent you from delegating to others at work? This is a good way to sabotage relationships and your confidence in having successful relationships.

Your emotions

16. **Anxiety.** When you stress, worry, or get anxious about an interview, a presentation, money, a family gathering, or any other situation, it can negatively affect your confidence and your level of success.

17. **Feeling Overwhelmed.** If you feel overwhelmed by the things you need to do, you may feel demotivated and may not complete them. Feeling overwhelmed can reduce your productivity and confidence and, therefore, your success.

18. **Overreacting with emotions.** When your "buttons" are pushed, you lose your objectivity and focus, and you get overwhelmed with anger, fear, hurt and other emotions. This can affect your ability to access positive emotions like confidence, and your ability to successfully achieve what you want.

19. **Taking things too personally.** Do you take other people's comments and feedback too much to heart? Do you feel really hurt by what others say? When you take things too personally, it can affect your confidence and success.

20. **Low motivation levels.** Do you lack the motivation to wake up, go to work, exercise, and take action on your goals and dreams? Lack of action leads to lack of success, which can negatively affect your confidence.

Your behaviour

21. **Procrastination.** When was the last time you put off doing something that you said you would do? Lack of action affects your success and therefore your confidence.

22. **Recurring unwanted patterns of behaviour.** Do you have a recurring pattern of behaviour with which you are unhappy, for example, settling for less than you deserve? Recurring patterns keep you stuck and limit your success and confidence.

23. **Sibling rivalry.** While healthy competition between siblings can help each other to excel and succeed, unhealthy competition can be very disempowering and damaging to your confidence and success.

24. **Indecisiveness.** When it comes to making decisions, do you hedge your bets, fear making a wrong decision, get confused, and then don't make a decision? Lack of decision leads to lack of action and lack of success. In turn, it reduces confidence.

25. **Inflexibility.** Is your current behaviour unsuccessful, yet you are not prepared to change to succeed? Being rigid and inflexible is a good way to keep repeating the same patterns, to keep being unsuccessful and to diminish your confidence.

26. **Bad habits.** Are you unhappy with any of your own bad habits such as smoking, drinking, nail-biting or overeating? These can reduce your confidence because they can affect your success in life.

27. **Catch-22.** Do you set yourself up so that regardless of

what you do, you lose either way? Whether you do or don't do what your partner, family, friend, colleague or manager asks, do they make you out to be wrong for it?

28. **Controlling others and situations.** Are you annoyed or frustrated when others don't do what you want them to do? Do you want to control other people and things beyond your control?

29. **Neediness.** Are you dependent on other people too much rather than relying on yourself to succeed? Is your neediness for love and attention pushing people away?

30. **Lack of skills.** Are there any technical skills that you need to learn in order to do well at work, a sport, or a hobby? Competence increases with confidence, and confidence increases with competence, as already discussed in Chapter 1.

31. **Lack of effective communication.** Do you have misunderstandings, disagreements, and conflicts with your loved ones and your colleagues at work? You need to learn new skills to increase your flexibility and effectiveness when communicating with other people.

Your environment

32. **Negative environment.** Are you surrounding yourself with negative people and situations? If you allow the negative environment to affect you, it can also sabotage your confidence and your success.

33. **External distractions.** Do you get easily distracted by computer games, television, other people's requests, or any other activities? These take your focus off your

priorities and goals in life and, hence, sabotage your success.

34. **Cluttered life.** Do you make your life so busy that you have no room for what you really want? Preoccupying yourself with other things keeps you from focusing on and having what you really want—it is self-sabotaging.

Your self-assessment quiz

All of the above can negatively impact on your confidence and on your success. If any of these are present for you, this could explain why you are not as confident and successful as you could be. Once you identify which of the above saboteurs are affecting your confidence and success, then you can more easily address them.

In Figure 2.3 you will find a self-assessment quiz to assist you to honestly identify the areas you need to address to stop the sabotage. Feel free to refer to the previous several pages for explanations. Go with the first answer that comes to you and be honest with yourself as you tick all the patterns that apply to you right now. For each of the sabotage patterns below think about and tick how often you run those patterns: never, sometimes, or always. If there are other patterns that you are using to sabotage yourself, you will find some blank rows in the self-assessment quiz where you can add in any extra ones you think of.

Number	Sabotage pattern	How often you run each pattern		
		Never	Sometimes	Always
	Your language			
1	Excuses			
2	Blame			
3	Beating up on yourself or negative self-talk			
4	Putting other people down			
5	Disempowering language			
	Your thoughts			
6	Self-doubts			
7	Limiting beliefs			
8	Internal conflicts			
9	Lack of clarity, direction, or goals			
10	Comparing yourself to others			
11	Lack of clear priorities			
12	Feeling unloved			
13	Feeling intimidated by other people			
14	Feeling stuck or trapped			
15	Not trusting other people			
	Your emotions			
16	Anxiety			
17	Feeling overwhelmed			
18	Overreacting with emotion			
19	Taking things too personally			
20	Low motivation levels			
	Your behaviour			
21	Procrastination			
22	Recurring unwanted patterns			
23	Sibling rivalry			
24	Indecisiveness			
25	Inflexibility			
26	Bad habits			
27	Catch-22			
28	Controlling others and situations			
29	Neediness			
30	Lack of skills			
31	Lack of effective communication			
	Your environment			
32	Negative environment			
33	External distractions			
34	Cluttered life			
	Other saboteurs			
35				
36				
37				
38				
39				
40				
	Total score			

Figure 2.3: Your self-assessment quiz

Now please add up all the ticks in each of the three columns. Notice the scores for each column. If you have a maximum score in the:

- **never** column—you are doing great and may need to do some work on any patterns in the other two columns.
- **sometimes** column—you have some work to do to stop those patterns of sabotage plus any other patterns you identified in the other two columns.
- **always** column—you have some serious work ahead of you, and if you honestly and consistently practice the exercises in this book, you will begin to see changes in your level of confidence and success.

Your scores will reflect the degree to which you are now sabotaging your confidence and your success. You may now also wish to refer to the scores for your current levels of confidence and success that you gave yourself for each area of your life in Chapter 1.

As you do that, notice whether the above patterns are sabotaging your confidence and success in all areas of your life or only some. Also, notice in which areas of life your confidence and success scores are highest and in which they are lowest.

Please note your observations below.

_____

_____

_____

_____

_____

_____

_____

_____

_____

Are you ready for the journey?

Now that you know the different ways that you are sabotaging yourself, are you happy to continue with your life as it is or are you ready to change those patterns? Please be honest with yourself. Awareness is the first step in your journey. The next step is your commitment to making the necessary changes, then working through the rest of the exercises in this book to empower yourself.

How to stop these patterns of sabotage is discussed in subsequent chapters of this book.

2.4   Summary

The key messages that we covered in this chapter include:

- Sabotage occurs any time you undermine yourself and your success.
- The more you run the same pattern of behaviour, the stronger that pattern becomes.
- Either you are in your comfort ("stale") zone or in the "growth" (learning) zone.

- Most people have had confidence at one time or another in their life and then "lost" it.
- There are many ways that people can sabotage themselves, either consciously or unconsciously.

2.5   *Your action journey*

What action will you now take after having read this chapter? Please note your action items from this chapter in your practice plan in Chapter 10 of this book.

3. Friend or foe?—Part 1

How your emotions affect your confidence and your success

Intuition will tell the thinking mind where to look next.

—Jonas Salk, Scientist

In the previous chapter, we discussed the many different ways that people can sabotage themselves. This chapter focuses on emotions and how they can be either our friend or foe—either empowering or disempowering us to have the confidence and success we desire.

3.1 What are emotions?

Are you in control of your emotions, or are your emotions controlling you? Do you ever witness or experience road rage, overwhelming frustration, or enormous guilt? Do you cry unstoppably, or feel immense hurt when someone says or does something? What if, instead, you reacted more appropriately to these everyday situations so that you lived each day to the fullest?

Emotions are feelings and our way of knowing that something feels comfortable or uncomfortable for us. Research demonstrates that feelings are caused by chemical reactions in our body and brain. Our feelings are, therefore, real rather than imagined. Paying attention to our emotions is very important.

All emotions are good, because they provide us with feedback as to whether something sits well with us or not. For example, if you are feeling frustrated when you communicate with others, because they don't understand you, that is your feedback to change what you are doing (and learn more effective ways of communicating) so that you stop feeling frustrated. (You will find more on effective communication techniques in Chapter 8).

Emotions are our friend because they help us to fully experience life. We have dozens of different emotions. Some are positive and empower us to feel, think, and act in positive ways. Other emotions are negative because they hold us back and can negatively impact on our personal and professional relationships. For example, think about the last time you spoke to someone who was angry. Were you listening to their message and what they were saying, or were you paying attention to their angry tone of voice? How did that impact on your relationship with them? Did it help them to build a stronger connection with you or not? Likewise, when you are angry with other people, it affects the connection and communication between you and them.

Some people who have been hurt in the past fear being hurt again. Hence, they can stop fully feeling their emotions as a way of protecting themselves from getting too close to others and being hurt again. Paradoxically, they are potentially hurting themselves by not being in a relationship they want because of the fear of being hurt again. In addition, people who are too disconnected from their emotions tend to have more health problems than those more in touch with their emotions, as we will discuss later in this chapter.

Positive emotions

There are many positive emotions. Examples of positive emotions include:

appreciation	anticipation	attraction	bliss
confidence	compassion	calm	curiosity
comfort	contentment	determination	drive
desire	elation	enthusiasm	empowerment
empathy	enjoyment	excitement	exhilaration
energy	ecstatic	eagerness	fulfilment
fun	hope	happiness	harmony
inspiration	joy	lust	laughter
love	motivation	pride	pleasure
peace	passion	relaxation	reassurance
satisfaction	success	serenity	zeal

Confidence and success are both positive emotions. While most people think of success as an end result (e.g. achieving a goal or completing a task), we can also feel the emotion of success as we think about our past and upcoming accomplishments and positive actions.

Negative emotions

There are also many negative emotions. Examples of negative emotions include:

abandonment	anxiety	anger	annoyance
angst	apprehension	betrayal	despair
wrath	dread	desperation	disappointment
depression	embarrassment	envy	frustration
fury	fear	greed	guilt
grief	hurt	hopelessness	humiliation
hatred	helplessness	irritation	jealousy
loss	loneliness	overwhelm	phobia
rage	regret	revenge	remorse
rejection	resentment	sadness	sorrow
shame	trauma	terror	vengeance

Many of these negative emotions can compromise our ability to fully access and feel confidence and success. You may have felt some or all of the above positive and negative emotions before.

Identifying the emotions you feel

As humans, we have dozens of different emotions so it is important for us to differentiate between the emotions we feel. Some emotions are stimulants (e.g. anger, fear, frustration, jealousy), while other emotions are suppressants (e.g. sadness, hurt, rejection, betrayal, disappointment). Emotions that are stimulants often have us feel "up," while those that are suppressants often have us feel "down".

Next time you have a pleasant or unpleasant experience, below is a simple way to identify the emotion(s) you are feeling around that experience:

- Close your eyes and reflect on that pleasant or unpleasant experience. As you think about that experience now, bring to mind any images and sounds around that experience. Then, get in touch with how you feel about that experience, e.g. you may say upset (even though this is a label rather than an emotion)
- Notice whether the emotion is positive or negative
- Are you feeling one or more emotion?
- Get in touch with the specific emotion or emotions you are feeling, e.g. sad

You can refer to the above lists to assist you if necessary. Make sure that you are feeling emotions rather than using labels or describing your behaviours, which are explained below.

Labels and Behaviours

Remember that emotions are feelings. People often use labels and say things like, "I feel..."

OK	good	awkward	foolish
judged	self-conscious	doubtful	empty
fine	alright	alive	alert
miserable	down	vulnerable	prosperous
upset	unloved	insecure	suspicious
light-hearted	sensational	amazing	fabulous
abundant	let down	on top of the world	positive
optimistic	pessimistic	lucky	carefree
trapped	worthless	negative	bad

Rather than being emotions, these are a combination of emotions and beliefs that they have labelled as one of the above. We will discuss beliefs in detail in the next chapter.

Also, keep in mind that there is a difference between an emotion and behaviour. A behaviour is an action or a behavioural response to a specific situation or person. The following are examples of behaviours or behavioural responses:

blaming	crying	indecisive	decisive
aggressive	arrogant	friendly	gentle
hostile	diplomatic	passive	assertive
timid	messy	deceitful	cooperative
disorganised	laid back	controlling	obsessive
talkative	rebellious	sociable	lazy
accepting	intimidating	tactful	addictive
organised	vigilant	admiring	distracted
quiet	giving	impulsive	disapproving
forgetful	compulsive	supportive	nurturing

While there may be emotions associated with some of the above behaviours, it is important to distinguish between emotions and behaviours so that you understand yourself better, and understand whether your reactions are emotional or behavioural. In addition, this will assist you to more easily use the appropriate techniques to change the disempowering reactions.

3.2   *Balanced versus out-of-proportion emotions*

There are two types of emotions: balanced emotions and out-of-proportion emotions. Our emotions are balanced when we feel an appropriate level of emotion in a particular situation. For example:

- if we are watching a sad movie, it is appropriate to feel sad
- if we are treated badly by someone, it is appropriate to feel angry
- if we are walking in a dark alley alone at night, it is appropriate to feel fear
- if we borrow something without asking, it is appropriate to feel guilty.

Sometimes we experience real threats or danger and our fight or flight response kicks in to protect us. As we feel danger, we either stay and fight it out (then feel anger after the event) or flee in fright (and feel fear afterwards). This is an appropriate response when faced with danger—it is your unconscious keeping you safe from physical and emotional harm.

Our emotions are out of proportion when our "buttons" are pushed, when we feel an overwhelming emotion or we react to a person or situation in a way that we are unhappy with. For example:

- crying unstoppably and feeling sad three days after watching a movie probably reflects sadness that is out

of proportion
- road rage is an example of out-of-proportion anger
- feeling afraid to do the things you really want to in life is a sign of out-of-proportion fear
- a child feeling overly guilty because her parents divorced and she blames herself for their break-up is a sign of out-of-proportion guilt

Some people express their emotions and others suppress them. People who suppress an emotion may internally let a situation fester and dwell on the events that have transpired. Either way, whether expressed or suppressed, out-of-proportion emotions prevent you from having the confidence and success you desire.

Emotions in context

In some contexts, positive emotions are appropriate, and in other contexts they may be inappropriate. Examples of the latter include:

- feeling attraction towards someone you don't wish to be attracted to, e.g. a married friend or colleague
- laughing at a serious meeting or family event

Likewise, in some contexts negative emotions are appropriate and in other contexts they may be inappropriate, as discussed above.

The context is important when considering whether an emotion is appropriate. In addition, the intensity of the emotion is the key to identifying whether an emotion is appropriate for the situation. For example, it is appropriate to feel really sad at a funeral. In contrast, feeling that same amount of sadness twenty years later suggests that the emotion is probably out of proportion.

While all emotions are always your friend, letting you know when something feels right or not for you, the context and intensity of the emotion will determine whether an emotion is *only* your friend or also your foe. Emotions become your foe when they hold you back from being, doing, and having what you want in life, and when they sabotage your confidence and your success. Some examples of when emotions become your foe include:

- if you have so much past hurt that you avoid getting into another relationship (even though you want one) for fear of being hurt again
- if you avoid going for the job or promotion you want because of thoughts of past rejection and fearing rejection again
- if you avoid giving presentations because of a big fear
- if you put others' needs ahead of your own because you feel really guilty for pursuing your dreams and goals
- if you have much past resentment that you avoid helping others because you resent them not helping you.

Your unconscious

There are two aspects to our mind—conscious and unconscious. Our conscious is the analytical and thinking aspect of our mind, while our unconscious is the feeling and intuitive aspect of our mind. All our memories and past conditioning are stored at the unconscious level. According to neuroscience, our unconscious programming defines at least 95% of our life experience, with our conscious contributing to only about 5%.

Emotions are also our link with the unconscious aspect of our mind. The unconscious is where our emotions reside, and when we listen to our emotions, we are listening to our unconscious.

The main role of your unconscious is to keep you safe and to protect you. For example, when you go to touch a hot pan on the stove, your unconscious protects you by sensing the heat, and you instantly pull your hand away. People who get burned second-guess or analyse their feelings and sensations rather than trusting them. Because the unconscious protects you it will also tell you when something does not feel right. This is why it is important to listen to and trust your unconscious. There have probably been times when you listened to your gut or intuition (your unconscious) and you were glad you did. And there have probably been times when you didn't listen to your unconscious and you wish you had.

The more our "buttons" are pushed, the more ready we are to deal with these. It is your unconscious letting you know that you are ready to address those emotions by making you aware of them.

Negative emotions can confuse you and prevent you from listening to your unconscious. For example, if you have un-resolved fear, it can prevent you from acting out of trust and following your intuition. Instead, the fear holds you back and can have you act against your intuition. When there is out-of-proportion fear, we make fear-based decisions rather than rely on our pure intuition. Once the out-of-proportion fear is addressed, we can more easily listen to our pure intuition and act upon it.

Bystander or go-getter—Which are you?

Out-of-proportion fear holds you back from taking action and fully participating in life. It is a major saboteur of confidence and success. Fear has you being a bystander and simply observing everyone and everything else and wishing you could do the things you want. Are you a go-getter and participating in life 100%, or simply a bystander watching life pass you by? On a scale of 0% to 100% below, where do you rate your participation in life right now? Place a cross on the scale below.

Bystander	Go-getter
0% participating	100% participating

As you look at that percentage, is that level of participation in life giving you the confidence and success you desire? Write "yes" or "no" below.

_____

3.3   Negative emotions as saboteurs

Out-of-proportion negative emotions often prevent you from fully accessing positive emotions. Hence, they can sabotage your confidence and success. If in some contexts you feel confident and others you do not (as discussed in Chapter 1), this could be because there are out-of-proportion negative emotions present in some situations, which are putting a lid or limit on your level of confidence.

Below are the top 5 ways to identify any possible negative emotions that you may need to address.

As you read through each one, make a note of any that apply to you right now, the emotions associated with each one, and how they prevent you from having the confidence and success you desire.

1. Overreacting to situations with emotions, e.g. road rage in traffic, feeling overwhelming sadness about world events, feeling really hurt by what you see in a movie.

_____

_____

_____

_____

2. Overreacting to people with emotion e.g. being very short-tempered, crying uncontrollably when others make comments about you, feeling really rejected when your ex-partner's name is mentioned, taking other people's comments too personally, having your "buttons" pushed, taking offence to things too quickly, someone "rubbing you up the wrong way."

_____

_____

_____

_____

3. Beating up on yourself too much or being overly critical or judgemental of yourself may mean you are angry with yourself, or feel guilty.

_____

_____

_____

_____

4. Finding it difficult to forgive other people for what has happened in the past may mean you are angry, resentful, or vengeful towards them.

_____

_____

_____

_____

5. Being surrounded by people with similar emotions to you. Like attracts like.

_____

_____

_____

_____

Your emotional check-up

Are your emotions appropriate or inappropriate? Do they empower or disempower you to succeed?

Think about the emotions you've felt over the past month and make a list of all the negative emotions below. You can refer to the previous pages in this chapter for a list of some common negative emotions. Next to each negative emotion, think about and write down the intensity of the negative emotion you felt and give it a score out of 10 (10 = really intense).

Negative emotion	Intensity (1 to 10)	Appropriate for situation?
e.g. Fear	8	No

Negative emotion	Intensity (1 to 10)	Appropriate for situation?

As you look at the above scores, next think about whether it was appropriate for you to react with that level of emotional intensity in that situation. Then write a "yes" or "no" in the last column above. Next, circle the "no" answers and notice the emotions that they relate to. These are the emotions that are out of proportion for you and are sabotaging your confidence and success in life.

If, instead of expressing your emotions, you internally let a situation fester or dwell on the event well after the event has occurred, think about those situations now. In the first column below, write down all those situations that have occurred in the past month. Next to each one, write down how you feel as you think about that situation now.

Really think about each of those situations, one at a time, and get in touch with the emotion(s) you feel about the situation. Write the name of the emotion(s) below. Is the intensity of the emotion(s) you now feel about that situation appropriate or not for the situation? Are you happy with your reaction to the situation? Write a "yes" or "no" in the last column below.

Situation	Negative emotion(s)	Happy with my reaction?
e.g. Colleague puts me down	*really angry, huge rejection*	*No*

Situation	Negative emotion(s)	Happy with my reaction?

Look at the above responses then circle the "no" answers and notice the emotions that they relate to. These are the emotions that you have been internally suppressing, which you need to address. Once addressed, those events will stop playing on your mind and you will be able to stop sabotaging your confidence and success in life.

The negative effects of negative emotions

While all emotions are good, if we hold onto negative emotions for too long and they remain out of proportion, they can create negative effects for our health and overall well-being. One of the negative consequences of suppressing or ignoring our emotions is poor health. There is more and more scientific research showing the link between negative emotions and our health and well-being.

According to research at Concordia University, for instance, harbouring bitterness for a long time can result in anger, which in turn, if strong enough, can affect physical health (including the metabolism, the immune system, and organ function). A 2013 study at Ohio University demonstrated that dwelling on negative events can increase inflammation levels in the body. Another piece of research at Ohio State University in 2013 demonstrated that loneliness negatively affects the immune system by increasing inflammation in the body. A study published in Psychological Science in 2013 examined the relationship between daily negative emotions and their impact on mental health a decade later. It showed that levels of negative emotions predicted anxiety and depression a decade after the negative emotions were originally measured.

If you are interested in learning more about how the mind–body connection works and how you can reprogram it for optimal health, please refer to the Appendix at the back of this book.

Given the possible negative impacts of negative emotions, it is important to let these go so that we can improve our health, well-being, and success in life. Addressing out-of-proportion negative emotions also assists us to fully access and feel positive emotions and have greater confidence and success. How to address negative emotions is the subject of Chapters 5 and 6 of this book.

3.4 Summary

The key messages that we covered in this chapter include:

- Emotions are feelings and our way of knowing that something feels comfortable or uncomfortable for us.
- There are two types of emotions: balanced emotions and out-of-proportion emotions.
- Emotions become our foe when they hold us back from having the confidence and success we desire.
- When there is out-of-proportion fear, we make fear-based decisions rather than relying on our pure intuition.
- Because there is more and more research showing the link between negative emotions and our health and well-being, it is important to address any out-of-proportion negative emotions to improve our health and success in life.

3.5 Your action journey

What action will you now take after having read this chapter? Please note your action items from this chapter in your practice plan in Chapter 10 of this book.

4. Friend or Foe?—Part 2

How your beliefs affect your confidence and your success

They are able who think they are able.

—Virgil, 70–19 BC, Roman poet

In the previous chapter, we discussed negative emotions and how they can be our foe. In this chapter, we focus on beliefs and how they, too, affect our confidence and our success.

4.1   *What are beliefs?*

Beliefs are what we wholeheartedly believe: what we know to be true about ourselves, our self-image, our abilities, other people, and the world around us. Beliefs are our convictions about what is possible, what we can or cannot do, and what we accept as true. Beliefs determine our reality. If our beliefs are positive (e.g. I am a successful person) they support us in creating success. If our beliefs are limiting (e.g. I can't succeed) then these can limit our success in life. Whatever we believe, whether positive or negative, becomes real, because it affects our thoughts, feelings, and behaviour, and how we respond to people and situations.

While many of our beliefs were developed during our child-hood, early schooling, and early adult life, they can significantly impact on our success today. Like emotions, our beliefs are stored at the unconscious level.

Empowering beliefs

While there are many possible empowering beliefs, here are some examples:

I am deserving of success	I deserve to be loved
I deserve to have money	I can do anything
I trust myself	I trust other people
I am a successful person	I have a healthy body
I get along well with people	People are good
I am a good person	Life is great
It is easy to learn	I can have anything I want

Empowering beliefs are our friend because they assist us to access more of our potential, support us to succeed, and help to grow our confidence.

Disempowering beliefs

Likewise, there are many possible disempowering beliefs. Some examples include:

I am not deserving of happiness, love, money, success, etc.	
I am not worthy	I need to be perfect/I am not perfect.
I don't trust myself	I don't trust other people
Fear of failure	Fear of success
Fear of rejection	Fear of being hurt
Fear of being alone	Fear of public speaking
I am not good enough	Fear of being judged

How limiting beliefs affect our confidence and our success

Any and all of the above disempowering beliefs can sabotage our confidence and success. This is because our beliefs are reflected in our behaviours. For example, if you have a fear of rejection, you may find yourself doing or saying things in an interview that have the other person respond with a "no," and so they reject you. We call these beliefs limiting because they limit your confidence and success. Limiting beliefs are your foe if they prevent you from being, doing, or having what you want in life.

Here are a few more examples of how limiting beliefs can affect your behaviour, confidence, and success:

- You stay in an emotionally abusive relationship because of a fear of being alone. This negatively affects your confidence and your ability to make objective decisions about your relationship and life.
- You stay in a job you hate because you believe you don't deserve better. This affects your confidence to change your job situation so you can be more successful in your career.
- You fear failure, so you overanalyse and second-guess yourself. This has you miss out on opportunities so you feel like you have failed again, which affects your confidence and success.

4.2   Identifying your limiting beliefs

Before you can address your limiting beliefs, you need to identify them. One way to identify any limiting beliefs is to look at your behaviour, because your beliefs are reflected in your behaviour (as in the above examples). Please keep in mind that these are simply examples, which may or may not be relevant to you.

Some people find it easier to identify their limiting beliefs as they go to do things, so the next exercise will assist you in this regard. For the next week, make a note in the following table of all the things you put off or avoid doing. Next to each activity, write down the thought(s) you had that had you avoid or put off doing that activity. Finally, what is the belief that sits behind that thought? It may help you to refer to the previous lists for examples of beliefs. Write this in the final column.

Activity	Thought(s)	Belief(s)
e.g. put off study	*e.g. what if I fail?*	*e.g. fear of failure*

Once you complete the exercise, look through your replies and notice the beliefs that have been holding you back from taking action. Is there a theme? Circle those beliefs now, please. These are currently limiting you, your confidence, and your success.

Excuses and beliefs

Most excuses reflect our unconscious limiting beliefs. Note below the excuses you made in the past week.

Excuse	Why I made that excuse
e.g. I am too tired to exercise	*e.g. feared achieving my goal weight, fear of success*

Excuse	Why I made that excuse

Next to each excuse, ask yourself why you made that excuse. Be honest and go with the first answer, even if it seems irrational. For example, when you said, "I am too tired to exercise," why did you make that excuse? Was it because you feared succeeding at achieving your goal weight, for example? As you read through the above, notice any similarities in your excuses and why you made them. Please circle any similarities you notice.

Negative self-talk and beliefs

Often your self-talk will reflect your unconscious beliefs. Negative self-talk also includes self-doubts, which reflect your limiting beliefs. When did you last question yourself, doubt yourself or your abilities? Over the coming week, note below any negative self-talk and self-doubts you have, and the beliefs associated with each.

Negative self-talk or self-doubt	Why I questioned or doubted myself
e.g. what if I can't do it?	*e.g. I can't trust myself*

Negative self-talk or self-doubt	Why I questioned or doubted myself

Then ask yourself, "Why did I question or doubt myself?" and go with the first answer. Write this next to each self-doubt above. As you read through the above, notice any similarities in your self-doubts and why you questioned or doubted yourself. Please circle any similarities you notice.

Beliefs and bad habits

We call unwanted habits "bad" habits because they are undesirable to us, and often we wish we could change them. There are many types of bad habits. Some examples include:

- Smoking
- Unhealthy eating, e.g. overeating, chocolates, junk food
- Unhealthy drinking, e.g. energy drinks, alcohol
- Distractions, e.g. TV, internet surfing, movies, online games
- Nail-biting
- Sleeping in, going to bed late
- Untidiness

Some of the above can be appropriate in moderation and when done for the right reasons. For example, watching TV to relax is appropriate, while watching TV every time you want to avoid doing what you said you would do is potentially a bad habit. Often limiting beliefs underpin bad habits. For example:

- Untidiness can be due to a limiting belief that "I am lazy," which is exhibited in the person's behaviour.
- Smoking cigarettes could be due to a limiting belief that "I can't stop smoking," which will prevent a person from changing that behaviour.
- Sleeping in and being unable to get up on time could be due to the limiting belief that "I can't discipline myself."

Over the coming week, note below any of your own bad habits and the beliefs associated with each one.

Bad habit	Why I have that habit

Bad habit	Why I have that habit

Ask yourself, "Why do I have that bad habit?" Go with the first answer. Write this next to each bad habit above. The above examples will assist you with this. As you read through the above, notice any similarities in your bad habits and why you have the habit(s). Please circle any similarities you notice.

As you read through the last four exercises, what patterns do you notice? Are there similar beliefs that hold you back? Make a note of these below.

_____

_____

_____

_____

_____

_____

_____

_____

_____

_____

4.3   *Insecurities and sabotage*

Sometimes we experience real threats or danger and our fight or flight response kicks in to protect us. As we feel danger, we either stay and fight it out or flee in fright. This is an appropriate response when faced with danger—it is our unconscious keeping us safe, as we discussed in Chapter 3.

If we perceive life situations as threatening to us, we will either respond in proportion or overreact to that perceived threat with our insecurities. Perceived threats are just that—

our perception and our interpretation that an event is a threat to us, even if there is no actual threat.

Perceived threats can include threats to:

- our comfort zone
- our identity and how we perceive ourselves
- our values and beliefs
- other people's success and behaviour
- our job or financial security
- our relationship or family

Our emotions and beliefs will determine how we respond to events and people and whether we feel safe or threatened. Any time we overreact to a perceived threat, we need to pay attention because our internal insecurities will feed any patterns of sabotage.

Look at the situations below. How do you react when:

- your partner argues or gets angry with you?
- you feel hurt, rejected, or betrayed by a loved one?
- your sibling gets a new partner, job, or achieves some other success?
- your friend does things that you wish you could do?
- your colleagues are promoted over you?
- people around you lose weight, buy a new house, go on holidays, or are generally happier than you?
- people around you feel threatened?

Is your response (your emotions, thoughts, and actions) to the above appropriate or out of proportion? Below are some common ways that people respond to perceived threats.

The controller.

When feeling threatened, the controller wants to take control of the situation or may get angry if they feel out of control. The controller may even exhibit verbal or physical bullying behaviour and/or may blame others for their anger and behaviour.

The over-protector.

When threatened, the over-protector will want to protect themselves and/or others. They may be a rescuer and take too much responsibility for other people. They may put up a protective wall to protect themselves from being vulnerable or being emotionally hurt.

The envier.

When threatened by others' success and achievements, the envier's "green-eyed monster" appears. They may covet what others have, may avoid contact with them, or go into a jealous rage. They may even put others' successes down and gossip negatively about them to make themselves feel better.

The drama queen.

When threatened, the drama queen makes a mountain out of a molehill and overreacts with emotion. The drama that they create reflects their own internal fears, out-of-proportion emotions, self-doubts, and insecurities.

The attention-seeker.

When threatened, the attention-seeker turns others' attention onto themselves and unconsciously asks, "What about me?"

They may ignore others' successes and talk about their own achievements instead. Their insecurities about themselves feed their need for attention from others.

The approval-seeker.

When threatened, the approval seeker bends over backwards to befriend the people they feel threatened by in an effort to gain their approval. They may revert to others' approval before making their own decisions. They may even make excuses for other people's negative behaviour in order to gain their approval.

The empowerer.

The empowerer rarely feels threatened by others. They are their own person, secure in themselves, seeing every life experience as an opportunity to learn and grow. They are supportive of others' successes and are genuinely happy for them.

Stop feeling threatened and insecure.

How you respond to other people's successes speaks volumes about you. As you consider the above responses, which ones can you honestly say apply to you? You can be more like the empowerer and stop feeling threatened and insecure by following the three steps below.

1. Be honest with yourself and acknowledge how you respond to perceived threats. Use the above categories as a guide. To assist you with this, think about the last five times one of your loved ones, friends, or colleagues had a success. Write these situations down.

Success event	My thoughts, feelings, and language	Category	Appropriate?
e.g. colleague promoted	e.g. they don't deserve it, jealous, gossiping negatively about them	e.g. envier	no

Next to each one, note how you responded to that person's success. What were you thinking, feeling and saying about their success? Which of the above categories reflected your response? Was your response appropriate, or did you overreact based on your own insecurities?

2. Identify the specific negative emotions and limiting beliefs that have you feel overly threatened and insecure in the above situations. You can refer to the exercises in this and the previous chapter to assist you with this and then list those below.

_____

_____

_____

_____

_____

_____

_____

_____

_____

_____

3. Address the areas you identified in Step 2 above so that you can feel more confident and successful instead. We will explain this in the subsequent chapters of this book.

Control versus trust

People who trust themselves also trust others and the flow of life. Therefore, they find no need to control people and situations. It is only people who have trust issues that feel the need to control others and situations. These people need to learn to trust themselves first so they can trust others.

How much do you trust yourself to make decisions that are right for you? When it comes to making decisions around relationships, career, finances, health, family, friends, or any other area of your life, how often do you second-guess, overanalyse, or doubt your decision?

Trusting yourself and your decisions is the key to success in life, because when you trust yourself you are listening to your unconscious, which is always protecting you. It is also important to act on your intuition rather than to question it or ignore it.

For example, a 2012 study by UCLA found that couples who

were most satisfied with their marriage four years later were those without any doubts about getting married prior to their wedding. In contrast, the ones with doubts were two and a half times more likely to divorce four years later.

This has also been my experience with clients. When asked when they first sensed something wasn't right in their relationship or at work, clients will be able to point to events years earlier and say that their intuition told them "to leave," for example, yet they stayed because it was comfortable. Years later, they are still in an unhappy relationship or career. Your unconscious always has the answers that are right for you.

The challenge for most people is to learn to trust themselves and to act upon their internal knowingness (their unconscious). If you lack total trust in yourself and wish you had more confidence and success in life, then you will need to address this belief also.

Now that you have identified the negative emotions and limiting beliefs that are holding you back from having the confidence and success you desire, it is important to be ready to let these go. The next chapter will assist you with this.

4.4   Summary

The key messages that we covered in this chapter include:

- Beliefs are what we wholeheartedly believe: what we know to be true about ourselves, our abilities, other people, and the world around us.
- Disempowering beliefs can sabotage our confidence and success because our beliefs are reflected in our behav-

iour.

- Most excuses, negative self-talk, self-doubts, and bad habits reflect our unconscious limiting beliefs.
- How you respond to other people's success speaks volumes about you.
- Trusting yourself and your decisions is the key to success in life.

4.5   *Your action journey*

What action will you now take after having read this chapter? Please note your action items from this chapter in your practice plan in Chapter 10 of this book.

Phase II

Transform your confidence

5. Empower yourself

Instant confidence and success

Man's mind, once stretched by a new idea, never regains its original dimensions.

—Oliver Wendell Holmes Jr., US Supreme Court Justice

Now that you have identified and become aware of your patterns of sabotage and of how you are sabotaging your confidence and success, it is important to have some tools to empower yourself to change how you think, feel, and act.

Before I share some of these simple and effective self-empowerment techniques with you, first you need to realise that some people continue to sabotage themselves despite their awareness of those patterns. Usually, this is as a result of negative emotions, limiting beliefs, and internal conflicts that are left unaddressed.

Cognitive dissonance theory also explains why people fail to stop sabotaging themselves. This theory states that people tend to seek out information that fits in with their existing beliefs, values, and behaviour, and ignore information that does not fit in with them. In turn, this continues to reinforce their existing beliefs, values, behaviours, and patterns of sabotage. Once negative emotions, limiting beliefs, and internal conflicts are addressed, the patterns of sabotage stop.

5.1   Are you ready and willing?

Is your current behaviour unsuccessful, yet you are not prepared to change to improve your success? Being rigid and inflexible is a good way to keep repeating the same patterns, to keep being unsuccessful, and to diminish your confidence.

Any change begins with your **willingness** and **readiness** to change. First, you need to identify which area(s) you are happy with and which you want to improve or change. In this book so far, you have worked through the exercises to assist you with identifying your patterns of sabotage. Which of these are you now ready to change? All, some, or none of these? You can make a note of these below.

Areas in my life and behaviours that I am totally happy with or wish to leave unchanged right now:

_____

_____

_____

Areas in my life or patterns of sabotage that I would like to improve or change right now:

_____

_____

_____

_____

The benefits of change

Next, think about how you will benefit from making those changes or improvements. How specifically will your life improve from stopping the patterns of sabotage? Think about the benefits to you rather than to other people. Will you:

- improve your self-confidence and motivation?
- create lasting and fulfilling relationships with people?
- be more successful and fulfilled in your career or business?
- discover and clarify your passion?
- achieve and maintain your ideal weight and optimal health?
- achieve some other benefit?

Note below all the benefits you will achieve from stopping the patterns of sabotage that you wish to change right now.

_____

_____

_____

_____

_____

_____

_____

Now that you can see some positive benefits to stopping your self-sabotage, it is time for you to decide if you would like to make this change. Only you can make this choice. Take a moment now to honestly ask yourself, "Am I ready to now make the above changes to empower myself?"

This is an important step because the techniques I am about to share with you will only make a difference and work for you if you **want** them to work—if you are **ready** to make the change for yourself. You need to have the **will** and the **desire** to make the change. Then, once the desire and will is there, the change is much easier.

5.2   Anticipation and anxiety

Anticipation is having an expectation or making a prediction about what will happen. We can expect that events (e.g. a meeting, a presentation) or tasks (e.g. study, report) will go well, or anticipate that things will not go well. Because our thoughts are linked to how we feel, any time we expect something to go well, we feel positive emotions (e.g. excitement) about that event or task. In contrast, when we expect something to not go well, we feel negative emotions (e.g. anxiety) about that event or task.

Anxiety is a feeling that can occur when we:

- anticipate or expect negative scenarios
- do negative 'what ifs' in our mind or expect worst case scenarios
- think about an event or a task not going well
- think about what we don't want to happen or what could go wrong
- are unsure or uncertain about what could happen

- worry, stress, or dread an event or task

As you think about upcoming events in the next month, do you have positive or negative expectations of them? List those upcoming events below, together with your expectation of how each event will go, and whether it is positive or negative.

Upcoming event	My expectation	Positive or negative?
e.g. presentation at work	e.g. What if I forget what to say?	negative
e.g. presentation at work	e.g. I speak confidently	positive

Circle any negative expectations in the above exercise. Notice whether your expectations of the above events are mainly positive or negative. The negative expectations about these events are probably causing worry or anxiety.

Likewise, as you think about upcoming tasks in the next month, do you have positive or negative expectations of how they will go? List the upcoming tasks below, together with your expectation of how each task will turn out and whether it is positive or negative.

Upcoming task	My expectation	Positive or negative?
e.g. study	*e.g. What if I fail the test?*	*negative*
e.g. study	*e.g. I feel calm and do well*	*positive*

Circle any negative expectations in the above exercise. Notice whether your expectations of the above tasks are mainly positive or negative. The negative expectations about these tasks are probably causing worry or anxiety.

Whether you expect a worst-case or a best-case scenario, either way your thoughts will become self-fulfilling. Our thoughts affect our behaviour, become self-fulfilling, and predict our future.

Scientific research has recently proven that the mind is unable to differentiate between what is vividly imagined and what is real. Separate research teams, at both Harvard University and Washington University, found that the same brain regions were activated (plus a few others) when subjects imagined the future and when they recalled the past.

According to research at the University of British Columbia, people who worry about workplace rejection or sabotage can bring it upon themselves; their worries can become self-fulfilling. The study showed that people who are paranoid about negative gossip or being snubbed by their peers sought out information about such behaviour. In the process, they were more likely to have angered and to have been rejected by their colleagues, confirming their fears.

Other studies found that people who focused on making good things happen were less likely to suffer from anxiety than those who focused on preventing bad things from happening. This is why it is important to program your thoughts and emotions for what you do want, so that you can create a positive self-fulfilling prophecy through your behaviour.

Visualisation made easy

Several techniques in this book are visualisation-based tools, where you are actively using your imagination to recall or imagine an experience. Some people think that visualisation involves clearly seeing or imagining pictures, people or events in their mind. Hence, they may find it challenging to visualise if they have a different way of doing the process.

Let me explain what visualisation is. It is a mental process of using some or all of your senses (seeing, hearing, feeling, tasting, and smelling) and/or self-talk to recall or create an experience in your mind. Mental rehearsal is another name for visualisation. Some people's visualisation will be more vivid than that of others. If, for example, the pictures you imagine are vague, fuzzy, or blurry that is perfect. If the pictures you image are clear, detailed, and sharp, that is perfect too. There is no right or wrong way when it comes to how you do the visualisation. What is more important is the result you have from the visualisation. When you achieve success with a visualisation exercise in this book that means you visualised perfectly—you achieved the result you set out to achieve. Let go of having to see things clearly during your visualisation—instead, enjoy the journey and the result.

Visualisation can be done using any, some, or all of the following:

- seeing pictures, including people, images, colours, shapes, and events
- hearing sounds, including other people's comments, music, and noises in your environment
- feeling emotions or sensations, including internal feelings and sensations, being touched or hugged by other people, and feeling good about people and events
- smelling scents and odours around you, other people, and the environment
- tasting food and drinks, etc.
- self-talk and thinking about things, people, and events.

For example, if I asked you to now close your eyes and remember the last time you were at a beach, notice what:

- pictures come to mind, e.g. seeing the blue sky

- sounds or voices you hear, e.g. hearing other people laughing
- feelings or sensations you feel, e.g. the warm sand between your toes
- self-talk you hear, e.g. thinking to yourself how relaxing it is to be away from work
- tastes you experience, e.g. the vanilla flavour from the ice cream you just had
- smells you notice, e.g. the salty air of the sea

Go ahead and now remember the last time you were at the beach. Notice any pictures, sounds, feelings, self-talk, tastes, and smells as you think about the last time you were at the beach. Notice how recalling that event puts you in a different state. For example, do you feel more relaxed than you did before closing your eyes? Notice how changing your thoughts affects how you think and feel. You may have even noticed how it impacts on your body. You may notice a slowing down of your breathing when you recall being at the beach. This is how your thoughts affect your feelings, bodily sensations, and functions. We call this the mind–body connection.

Banish anxiety

The best way to enjoy an upcoming event or task is to focus on what is within your control. As discussed in Chapter 1, there are three things that you can personally control in any situation—how you think, feel, and act (including how you respond to and influence other people in those situations). If you focus on other people and events or circumstances beyond your control, you may get frustrated. When you focus on what is within your control, you feel happier and more in charge.

Here is a powerful technique to help you focus on what you want (and on what is within your control) so that you enjoy your next event or task more. It is an effective visualisation technique that is easy to use. However you visualise is perfect— the key is that you feel positive emotions at the end of this process.

1. Think about your next event or task (e.g. a meeting)— where, when, and with whom it will be.

2. Be clear about your outcome for that meeting. What would you like to achieve at that meeting (e.g. reach an agreement)?

3. With your eyes closed, imagine a movie screen in front of you and see yourself in the movie like an actor or actress at that future meeting with the other person, at the date and location of your meeting.

4. As you watch the movie, see that meeting turn out exactly as you would like it to be, hear the conversations you would like to hear, feel exactly how you would like to feel, and ensure your self-talk is positive about how your meeting will go. Make sure you focus on what is within your control during that meeting so that you easily achieve your outcome for that meeting.

5. Notice how you now feel better about that meeting when you focus on what you want, and how you now look forward to it. Open your eyes feeling confident and motivated about your meeting.

Take a moment now to do this exercise for an upcoming event or task and visualise it being a success. Highly successful people and athletes use this technique to visualise a successful event or game. Research shows that those athletes who visualise rehearsing and having a successful game do as well on game day as do athletes who have physically rehearsed and practiced prior to the game! After visualising a successful event or task, you will probably notice that you are also feeling more confident and motivated about this event or task.

5.3   How to achieve instant confidence

As discussed in Chapter 2 and in the previous section, every thought we think affects how we feel and how we act. Therefore, if you want to feel a certain way, all you need to do is to remember a time in the past when you felt that way. For example, if you want to feel confident to rehearse a presentation right now, all you need to do is to remember a time in the past when you felt confident about anything and you will feel confident right now about your presentation too.

Take a moment now to go back to Chapter 1. Revisit the areas of life you wrote down and the scores you gave yourself for confidence in each of those areas. You may notice that your level of confidence is different for different areas of life. You can use this to your advantage now to access the confidence you feel in one context, so that you feel the same level of confidence in other contexts too.

You can also feel instant confidence using the simple process below to set up an anchor that lasts. Simply put, an anchor is when two things are linked together in your brain—a stimulus (e.g. see a red traffic light) and a response (e.g. stop at a red traffic light).

1. **Choose a spot** to set up the anchor somewhere on your

body. Pick a unique spot that you can easily access that you would not normally touch. For example, handshakes are too common, so you may wish to pick something more unique, such as a knuckle, a spot on your elbow, or pressing two fingers together. Remember to keep the anchor simple so that you can easily replicate it.

2. **Think of a specific time** in the past when you felt confident. Choose a specific time in the past when you felt that emotion strongly so that you can capture the intensity of that emotion in your chosen spot.

3. **Get ready** to set up the anchor. Remember that you want to start pressing the chosen spot the moment you start to feel confidence, and keep it pressed until just after you feel the peak of that confidence.

4. **Set up the anchor**. You may like to close your eyes or keep them open, whichever makes it easier for you to remember a specific time when you felt really confident. As you remember a specific time in the past when you really felt the confidence, go back to that time now in your mind. See what you saw at the time, hear what you heard at the time, and feel the confidence you felt at the time. As you start to feel that confidence, press your chosen spot and hold onto it until the confidence peaks. Really feel the confidence as it peaks. The moment you feel that the intensity of the confidence begins to drop, let go of the anchor.

5. **Wait** a few moments and think about something different. Now test your anchor by pressing it again in the same spot and with the same intensity as before. Notice how you feel the confidence that you anchored in that spot!

Take a moment now to set up your own anchor using these steps. Your anchor now gives you a choice as to how you feel at any moment, and helps you to access confidence at any time you choose.

To protect your anchor so it lasts, avoid using it when you feel strong negative emotions (e.g. anger, fear, hurt, rejection). It is best to resolve these negative emotions and any limiting beliefs from the past (which we will discuss in the next chapter). Otherwise, if you use your anchor when you feel those negative emotions or limiting beliefs, you could weaken it, negate it completely, or even indirectly create an anchor with those negative emotions or limiting beliefs.

You can also top up your anchor and make it stronger. Any time in the future when you feel confidence, you can add it to your existing anchor (you only need to use step 4 above). You can even set up more than one anchor: one for each positive emotion you want to feel at any time. Make sure you remember which anchor is for which emotion.

Resource anchor

Alternatively, you can create a resource anchor and put four or five different positive emotions in the one spot. Any time you use that anchor, you will feel a combination of those positive emotions at the same time.

To set up a powerful resource anchor, simply follow the steps below.

- Choose the four or five positive emotions you would like to feel more often. You can refer to Chapter 3 for a list of positive emotions. Make sure you choose four or five positive emotions that you have felt strongly in the past. For example, you might choose confidence, motivation, energy, and joy.

- One at a time, anchor each of those chosen emotions in the same place, using the steps above. For example:
    - Use steps 1 to 5 to anchor confidence in a knuckle
    - Use steps 1 to 5 to anchor motivation in the same knuckle
    - Use steps 1 to 5 to anchor energy in the same knuckle
    - Use steps 1 to 5 to anchor joy in the same knuckle
- Any time in the future when you want to be more resourceful, you simply use your anchor to feel the combination of positive emotions that you anchored in that spot. You can take a moment now to set up your resource anchor.

Imagine now being in control of your emotions, accessing confidence, motivation, energy, and any other positive emotion at any time you choose, and enjoying far greater success.

Empowering language

The language you use will either empower or disempower you, and will either increase or decrease your confidence. You cannot not influence yourself. Every word you speak and every thought you have has the potential to affect your confidence in that moment. For example, imagine you are feeling confident at work and then your colleague asks you to do something new. If in response to that request you say, "I don't know how to do that," without even working out how you could do it, that could undermine your confidence.

Words are very powerful, so it is important to learn to empower ourselves through our language. Often our language will reflect our beliefs. Once we change any limiting beliefs, this will be reflected in the language we use. We will discuss how to change our limiting beliefs in the next chapter. In the meantime, here are some empowering words you could use to replace potentially disempowering ones and begin to reprogram your thinking.

Potentially disempowering words	Empowering words
no	yes
try	make sure
don't	do
can't	can
should	could
have to	want to
impossible	possible
must	desire to
need to	want to
won't	will

Because we influence ourselves and others by what we say, do, and think every day, we may as well do it in empowering ways. For example, instead of saying, "It is impossible," you could say, "It is possible," then work out how to do the task at hand. Remember that if you look for an obstacle, you will always find one. If you look for a solution, you will find it too. Audrey Hepburn said it well when she said, "Nothing is impossible, the word itself says I'm possible!"

In addition to words, the phrases we use can be disempowering, too. Below you will find examples of common phrases people say and how they can sabotage our confidence and success.

Notice if you use any of these yourself.

Phrase	How it can sabotage your confidence and success
He doesn't like me.	You are assuming that the other person does not like you without having any proof. You are unable to read their mind. If you assume they don't like you, it may affect your confidence unnecessarily and sabotage a potentially successful relationship.
She **makes** me angry.	You are blaming the other person for how you feel and giving away your power to them, instead of taking responsibility for your own feelings. Blame keeps you stuck and sabotages your success.
I failed this test; that **means** I will fail again.	You are equating a past experience to a future experience and assuming that the past will be repeated in the future. This expectation can become self-fulfilling and sabotage your success and confidence.
I **must** do this. I **have to** do it. I **should** do it.	You are doing something out of obligation or need rather than want. This may lead to ill feelings for having to do it, so you may not be motivated to do it. You may sabotage the task through inaction, which in turn negatively affects your confidence.
I **can't** do that.	You are telling yourself that you can't and because your unconscious is listening to your self-talk, it will act upon it. Your self-talk will affect your ability to do it and will sabotage your confidence and your success.
I **never** get what I want. This **always** happens to me.	You are generalising that one or several events mean that the same thing will happen consistently in the future, too. This expectation can become self-fulfilling and sabotage your success and confidence.

Phrase	How it can sabotage your confidence and success
I have done **every-thing** to lose weight.	You are generalising—that one or several things that you have done means that there is nothing else you can do. This assumption could have you give up and hold you back from taking further action, sabotaging your success and confidence.
I **am** **not** **good** **enough**. She is **better** **than** me. I **want** **more** success. I need to **lose** weight / make **more** money.	You are comparing yourself or your current situation to something or someone else. If the comparison is invalid (e.g. comparing yourself to an expert with decades more experience), based on unrealistic expectations (e.g. being a perfectionist) or disempowering (e.g. using unhealthy waif-thin people as a role model) then you are sabotaging your confidence and your success.

Make a note below of the phrases you use often. The words in bold will assist you with identifying this in your language.

_____

_____

_____

_____

_____

_____

_____

Empowering questions

The questions you ask yourself will either empower or disempower you. As discussed in previous chapters, how you speak to yourself will affect how you feel and, therefore, your behaviour. Below are empowering questions you can ask yourself to obtain a different perspective on those of the above phrases you may be using. Asking yourself the questions below will help you to obtain a more solution-focused perspective on your current situation in life, to take action, and to stop sabotaging yourself.

Phrase	Empowering questions to inspire you to take action
He doesn't like me.	How do I know he doesn't like me? Do I have any real proof, or am I reading too much into what he says and does, and his facial expressions?
She **makes** me angry.	How am I choosing to allow her to make me feel angry? How could I choose to feel instead? How can I stop giving away my power to her and take control of how I feel?
I failed this test; that **means** I will fail again.	How does failing this test mean that I will fail again? Have I ever failed at something then succeeded the next time? How could I succeed next time by thinking differently and by taking different action?
I **must** do this. I **have to** do it. I **should** do it.	What would happen if I didn't do it? What would happen if I did do it? What would happen if I wanted to do it? What wouldn't happen if I wanted to do it?
I **can't** do that.	What prevents me from doing it? What would happen if I could do it? What wouldn't happen if I could do it?

Phrase	Empowering questions to inspire you to take action
I **never** get what I want. This **always** happens to me.	Never? When was there a time I did get what I want? Always? When was there a time when that did not happen in my life? What do I want to happen instead next time?
I have done **every-thing** to lose weight.	Everything? Have I really done everything to lose weight? What else have I not considered to lose weight safely? What else could I do to lose weight safely?
I am **not good enough**. She is **better** than me. I want **more** success. I need to **lose** weight / make **more** money.	Compared to who or what? Is my comparison valid? Am I comparing myself with my past performance or with an expert? Is my comparison realistic? Is my comparison safe and healthy? How does my current performance compare to my past performance? How could I further improve this?

Enjoy using and practising the techniques in this chapter to empower yourself for instant confidence and success. In the next chapter, we will cover more techniques to further assist you.

5.4   Summary

The key messages that we covered in this chapter include:

- Any change begins with your willingness and readiness to change.
- Whether you expect a worst case or a best case scenario, either way your thoughts will become self-fulfilling.
- You can banish anxiety by visualising a successful event or task.

- You can access instant confidence by setting up and using an anchor.
- Using empowering language and asking empowering questions, assists you to obtain a solution-focused perspective on your situation so that you can take action and be more successful.

5.5   *Your action journey*

What action will you now take after having read this chapter? Please note your action items from this chapter in your practice plan in Chapter 10 of this book.

6. Stop pushing my buttons!

Lasting confidence and success

Until you are happy with who you are, you will never be happy with what you have.

—Zig Ziglar

In this chapter, we share techniques to help you manage your emotions and beliefs for ongoing confidence and success.

6.1 Addressing negative emotions

As covered in Chapter 3, we have both positive and negative emotions. When negative emotions are out of proportion for us, we can overreact to people and situations. Think of out-of-proportion emotions like a dormant volcano—they can lie dormant only for so long. At some point, the pressure deep down inside builds up and has to erupt. It is just a matter of time before people and situations trigger the "volcano" to erupt with emotion.

When emotions are unaddressed, our "buttons" can be pushed. Remember that people can only push your "buttons" if you have "buttons" to be pushed. They are your "buttons" and only you can address them. When you address your "buttons," you will stop overreacting to what people say and do and you will deal with life more objectively. Rather than being controlled by your emotions, you will be in control of your emotions.

Instant calm

Negative emotions can have you feel out of balance, uncomfortable, or stuck and dwelling on and reliving past events. By putting yourself in a calm frame of mind, you can manage negative emotions effectively. Here is a quick way that you can stay calm until you address the past emotions fully at the unconscious level:

1. Sit comfortably on a chair and pick a spot in front of you, above eye level, that you can look at comfortably, e.g. a picture on a wall in front of you.
2. As you focus on that spot, keeping your head still, start to notice everything around you in your peripheral vision, e.g. the furniture either side of you, pictures on the walls, people around you.
3. Continue focusing on that spot for one to two minutes (keeping your head still and your eyes on that spot), while being aware of everyone and everything around you the whole time.
4. Notice how you feel being aware of everything and everyone around you and notice how it centres and calms you.

Practice this around people to manage your reaction to them. Practice this in your environment to manage how you think and feel as you action tasks. You can use this technique while in meetings, at your computer, doing any task, with other people or on your own, and any time you wish to feel calm.

Letting go of emotions about recent events

If you have had a recent argument or disagreement with your partner, family, friend, colleague, or manager, the technique below will assist you with changing your perspective on that recent situation and stop if from affecting you. It is a good way to diffuse emotions on **recent** events and situations, rather than letting them fester and continuing to be upset by them.

By getting a different perspective on the event, you will learn from it and feel better about the situation and towards the person involved. It is important to learn from past emotions, as they are there to teach us about ourselves. Once we learn from those emotions, the purpose for holding onto those emotions disappears.

Follow these steps to change how you feel about a specific event that involves another person:

1. Think about a specific recent event where another person was involved, e.g. a disagreement with the manger last week.

2. Sit down comfortably, close your eyes, and in your mind take yourself back to that specific event now.

3. See that whole event, looking through your own eyes (Position 1 in the diagram below), seeing the other person in front of you in that event. Notice how you think and feel in that situation as you look at that person through your own eyes in that situation. Observe the emotions you feel.

4. Now, float out of your body and into the other person's body. Imagine you are the other person (Position 2 in the

diagram below). See the whole event looking through their eyes, back at you in that event. Notice how you think and feel as you are in their shoes in that situation. Get in touch with the emotions you feel as you look through their eyes.

5. Next, float out of the other person's body up to the ceiling and imagine yourself as an objective observer on the ceiling looking through the eyes of the objective observer (Position 3 in Figure 6.1). Observe the whole event from above, seeing you and the other person in that specific event below. Notice how you now think and feel about the situation as you look at it from an objective observer's point of view.

Figure 6.1: The situation from an observer's point of view

6. As you objectively observe that event, ask yourself, "What can I learn from this situation that will assist me to let the emotions go now?" Go with the first answer that comes to you and make sure that it is a positive learning (without any "not," "can't", "don't," "no," "won't," "must," "have to," or "try"). A good way to state a positive learning is to begin it with "I can," "I am," or "I will."

Examples of positive learnings include:
- **I can** trust myself.
- **I am** a good person.
- **I will** be myself.

Examples of negative learnings include:
- I **can't** trust other people.
- That person is **bad**.
- I **won't** do that again.

7. Once you have the positive learning, float back down into your body (Position 1) and open your eyes. Notice how you now think and feel about that situation. Repeat this process if necessary. It is important to fully learn from events in order to fully let go of the emotions.

Now it is your turn to practise this exercise. First, choose a situation that you feel upset about that includes you and another person. Follow the above steps, and once they are complete, write down your positive learning below.

_____

_____

_____

6.2   Addressing limiting beliefs

As mentioned in Chapter 4, most excuses, self-doubts, and self-talk are based on our beliefs, so the best way to permanently stop the self-doubts, excuses, and negative self-talk is to change our limiting beliefs.

Affirmations versus beliefs

Many people think that by using affirmations they can change their negative self-talk. Affirmations are positive statements that people write out or say to themselves. Often they reflect what that person aspires to be, do, or have. For example, "I can do anything", "I allow an abundance of money to flow to me", or "I am fit and healthy." Beliefs are what we truly believe with all our heart about ourselves, other people, and the world around us. For example, "I believe I can do anything I set my mind to" or "I am worthy of success."

To affirm or to believe?

Our beliefs are reflected in our behaviour. It is more powerful to be congruent with what we believe because then our beliefs will automatically and unconsciously be reflected in our actions; they will drive our behaviour. Often people with limiting beliefs (e.g. "I am not good enough," fear of failure or success, "I can't make enough money") may feel the need to use affirmations to compensate for those limiting beliefs. People who have solid and congruent empowering beliefs feel little need for affirmations because their empowering beliefs are so strong they unconsciously act upon them. When we truly believe, affirmations become obsolete.

Our unconscious beliefs prevail

Our beliefs are stored unconsciously and affirmations are statements that people say on a conscious level. Any time we do not fully believe what we affirm, our unconscious beliefs will always win. Any time our affirmations are in conflict with what we believe, our unconscious beliefs prevail. For example, if a person says, "I live each day with joy and happiness," and if they have unconscious beliefs such as "I am not good enough," and "I don't deserve to be happy," and if they have out-of-proportion sadness, those limiting beliefs and the emotion of sadness will prevent them from being happy long-term despite the affirmation.

If you find yourself using affirmations and they are not helping you to create the relationship, career, health and life you desire, it is time to identify and address your unconscious limiting beliefs and negative emotions. Only once any limiting beliefs and negative emotions are addressed will affirmations work effectively, because then the person affirming will be congruent; they will believe and will truly feel what they are affirming. It is only then that positive affirmations can reinforce our empowering beliefs.

In Chapter 4, we discussed beliefs in detail, and you also identified some limiting beliefs that are sabotaging you now. Below are a couple of techniques that you can use to start to change those limiting beliefs now.

A solution-focused perspective

You can use the process below to assist you to obtain a different and solution-focused perspective on any limiting belief. Begin by thinking of a specific limiting belief you have right now. You may like to refer to the exercises in Chapter 4 to assist you. If you have more than one limiting belief, repeat this process separately for each one.

The key to making this process work for you is to read each question one at a time and to fully consider and think about each of them. Only then move on and ask yourself the next question. While some questions may seem unusual or confusing, they are designed that way to empower you. For simplicity, "the problem" below refers to the limiting belief you are working on.

1. What is the problem?
   (pause and really think about and get in touch with the limiting belief you chose and how you think and feel)

2. How did I participate in the problem with my thoughts, feelings, and actions?
   (pause and fully consider this question)

3. How could I fail at having the problem?
   (pause and fully consider this question)

4. How couldn't I not resolve this problem?
   (pause and fully consider this question)

5. What do I now choose as my solution?
   (pause and fully consider this question)

6. How could I make the solution to this work?
   (pause and fully consider this question)

7. How can I now feel the difference, knowing the solution and taking action towards it?
(pause and fully consider this question).

Once you have fully thought about these questions, take a moment to stand up and walk into a different room. When you return, ask yourself and fully consider the following questions:

1. How are things different now and into my future?
(pause and fully consider this question)

2. How do I feel about that? Make sure it is an emotion rather than a label or behaviour (you can refer to Chapter 3 to assist you).
(pause and fully consider this question)

Notice the different perspective that this has given you. If necessary, feel free to repeat this process again until you feel a positive emotion at the end of the process. Otherwise, you can use the same process for other limiting beliefs you wish to change.

This time consider the empowering beliefs that you would like to have so you can be as confident and successful as you want to be. You may wish to refer to Chapter 4 in this book for examples to assist you. Write these below.

_____

_____

_____

_____

_____

_____

_____

_____

_____

_____

_____

Because your mind is unable to differentiate between what is real and what is imagined, you can mentally rehearse having the above empowering beliefs, and the confidence and success you have as a result. Simply follow the steps below to mentally rehearse each new belief separately.

1. Choose one empowering belief from your list above.
2. Remind yourself of the location of your resource anchor (please refer to Chapter 5 in this book). You will need your resource anchor in Step 8 below.
3. Close your eyes and imagine a movie screen in front of you.
4. See yourself in the movie, like an actor or actress, with the empowering belief you chose. Use your imagination to notice how it positively impacts on your confidence and your success from now and into the future.
5. Make sure you have a picture of yourself in the movie, with any sounds, feelings, self-talk, tastes, and smells associated with it.
6. Intensify all of these senses and the self-talk as you watch yourself in the movie and really feel how that feels.

7. Feel the positive emotions (including confidence) you feel as you watch yourself in the movie. Turn up these positive emotions (imagine you are turning up an internal dial) to intensify the emotions.
8. Add the positive emotions you are now feeling to the spot you set up for your resource anchor.
9. Open your eyes feeling confident.

Repeat this process separately for each empowering belief on your list above. To reinforce this feeling any time in the future, fire off your resource anchor.

6.3 Resolving internal conflicts

In addition to limiting beliefs, internal conflicts can also limit you and your success. Are you sending mixed signals to your loved ones, colleagues, or friends? Do you experience confusion about whether or not you want to be in a job or work for yourself? Are you in two minds about whether a relationship with a partner is for you?

Fence-sitting foe

Any time you sit on the fence and are indecisive about what you want, this could signify that you have an internal conflict. Internal conflicts can pull you in different directions. For example:

- whether to stay single or get into a relationship
- whether to work for an employer or start your own business

- whether to seek love or not because of not feeling worthy of it

If you have your feet in both camps about what you want and are not fully committing to either one, you will never fully achieve either one. Hence, fence-sitting is your foe.

Inner conflict can drain your energy and motivation, as well as sending mixed signals to other people. It is also important to identify and resolve any inner conflicts so that you are congruent about what you want and you stop changing your mind. Once you make a congruent decision about what you really want, you will be fully committed to that course of action and will more easily follow through and achieve it. In turn, this will enhance your confidence and success.

Identifying conflicts

You can identify any of your own conflicts by using these common signs of potential inner conflict as a guide:

- Acting against or second-guessing your inner feelings, e.g. your gut feeling is to say "no" and you say "yes" instead.
- Contradicting yourself in what you say, e.g. saying, "I want to go for the promotion, but I'm not sure."
- Disagreeing with yourself, e.g. your internal dialogue says, "I want to be loved" one minute and "I don't deserve love" the next minute, thus creating confusion about what you really want.
- Saying things like "a part of me wants to do this, but a part of me doesn't" or "I am in two minds about it."

While often these signs can be subtle, the people around you will pick up on these cues unconsciously and will respond accordingly. Your uncertainty about what you want will be reflected in their uncertainty towards you, the relationship, or the job.

Over the next week, pay attention to your self-talk, your verbal communication, and your behaviour. Note below if it is consistent or if you notice any internal conflicts. You can use the common signs above to assist you with this.

_____

_____

_____

_____

_____

_____

_____

_____

_____

_____

Reaching agreement with yourself

Once you identify the internal conflict, it is important to resolve it by reaching agreement with yourself. An internal conflict can take a number of forms. The most common ones are:

- Internal confusion within yourself about how to have more than one option at the same time e.g. be in a relationship (option 1) while also having your own independence (option 2).
- Internal debate with yourself about which decision to make e.g. work for an employer (decision 1) or start your own business (decision 2).

Some conflicts are minor and can be very quickly addressed. Others are deep-seated conflicts. The exercises below will assist you with minor conflicts.

First, think about the conflict you have identified and chosen to work on. What type of conflict is it? Note the type of conflict and the details of the conflict below.

_____

_____

The exercise below will assist you with reaching a decision that is right for you. Ask yourself the following questions and notice the reply that instantly comes to mind.

- What specifically am I seeking from option/decision 1 (e.g. working for an employer, being in a relationship)?

_____

_____

_____

- What specifically am I seeking from option/decision 2 (e.g. starting my own business, having my independence)?

_____

_____

_____

- What is my outcome, objective, or purpose (one or two words only) for option/decision 1 (e.g. working for an employer, being in a relationship)? Examples of an outcome, objective, or purpose include fun, inner peace, contribution, love, and abundance.

_____

- What is my outcome, objective, or purpose (one or two words only) for option/decision 2 (e.g. starting my own business, having my independence)?

_____

- How similar are the above two outcomes, objectives, or purposes to me?

_____

_____

- What is the most appropriate way for me to now achieve the above outcome, objective, or purpose? Go with the first answer.

———————————————————————————

———————————————————————————

———————————————————————————

Next, visualise yourself in the future having what you want and how you achieve your outcome, objective, or purpose— notice the positive images, sounds, feelings, tastes, smells, and self-talk around taking action on the above decision.

Simply follow the steps below to mentally rehearse a successful future for yourself.

1. Close your eyes and imagine a movie screen in front of you.
2. See yourself in the movie, like an actor or actress, making the above decision now and the benefits to you now and into the future.
3. Make sure you have a picture of yourself in the movie, with any sounds, feelings, self-talk, tastes, and smells associated.
4. Intensify all of these senses and the self-talk as you watch yourself in the movie, and really feel how that feels.
5. Feel the emotions you feel as you watch yourself in the movie. Notice the positive images, sounds, feelings, tastes, smells and self-talk around your decision.
6. Open your eyes feeling confident about your decision.

7. Then ask yourself, "What steps do I want to take to achieve that?" Write these steps down below then set a goal and action your plan, which we will discuss in detail in Chapter 7.

You can repeat the above process to work through any other minor conflicts separately. This will help you to move forward decisively with consistent thoughts, feelings, and actions. Once those conflicts are resolved, you will have the confidence, clarity, and focus to create exactly what you desire in your life.

To address the negative emotions associated with all past events, all limiting beliefs, and deep seated internal conflicts, please refer to the Appendix in this book for details.

Enjoy using and practising the techniques in this chapter to empower yourself to have more confidence and success. In the next chapter, we will assist you with getting even more clarity, direction, and certainty about your future.

6.4   Summary

The key messages that we covered in this chapter include:

- People can only push your "buttons" if you have "buttons" to be pushed. Once you address your "buttons," they stop being pushed.
- By putting yourself in a calm frame of mind, you can manage any negative emotions effectively.
- Once you have a different perspective on an event, you can learn from it and feel better about the situation and the person involved.
- By obtaining a different and solution-focused perspective on any limiting belief, you can change it and then replace it with an empowering belief that strengthens your confidence and success.
- Internal conflicts can pull you in different directions. Therefore, it is important to reach agreement with yourself so you can confidently take action to achieve the success you desire.

6.5   Your action journey

What action will you now take after having read this chapter? Please note your action items from this chapter in your practice plan in Chapter 10 of this book.

7. Creating a certain and confident future

How to have exactly what you want, when you want it!

Obstacles are those frightful things you see when you take your eyes off your goal.

—Henry Ford

The uncertainty created by patterns of sabotage is the main reason preventing people from having clarity, direction, confidence, and success in life. Once you address and fully let go of all your past patterns of sabotage, it will be easier for you to create a certain and confident future for yourself. With certainty comes confidence in yourself and your ability to achieve what you desire.

7.1 You already know what you want

When I ask people what they want, I often hear them say, "I don't know what I want." Yet, you already know what you want. You already have all the answers that you seek, inside of you right now. When you address the negative emotions, limiting beliefs, and internal conflicts we discussed in the previous chapters, you become aware of exactly what you want. A clarity emerges from within you; all you need is some guidance to discover the answers that already lie within—the answers that are right for you. The exercises in this book so far would have helped you to gain greater clarity.

Give yourself permission to have it

Perhaps you are aware of exactly what you want, yet you are doing nothing about it. Maybe you want to change careers, start a business, get into a new relationship, or reach a health goal. Yet these remain unfulfilled dreams waiting to be turned into a reality.

Any time you make excuses for not taking action towards your dreams, you are excusing yourself from having what you want. These excuses can take the form of limiting beliefs, as we already discussed. For example, do you believe that you are worthy, deserving, and good enough to have what you really want? If so, then you just need to give yourself permission to have what you want and start taking action towards it. If not, you will need to address those beliefs (as we discussed in the previous chapters) so that they stop limiting you from having what you really want.

Stop sitting on the fence

Decide what you want and follow through on it. Stop hedging your bets either way just in case. These are often internal conflicts that we discussed in the previous chapter. Any lack of commitment to what you really want will be transmitted as mixed signals to people around you. Once you make a commitment to yourself and what you really want, you will start to attract the people and resources to assist you with having it. Until then, your success will be mixed.

Go for the best and forget the rest

Avoid settling for second best. Know what you really want and then avoid compromising yourself. For example, if you want a new job that satisfies eight criteria, avoid settling for a job that only meets two of your criteria, and telling yourself or thinking that "it is better than nothing" or "at least it is a job." Negative emotions, limiting beliefs, and internal conflicts often cause people to settle for less than what they really want. Never settle for less than what you really want, as any time you do, you send a very disempowering message to your unconscious—that you do not deserve to have what you really want. When you totally believe in yourself and your abilities, you have the inner certainty to only go for what you really want.

Filling the vacuum

Once the patterns of sabotage are addressed, it effectively creates a vacuum in your mind, which is waiting to be filled. As the old adage goes, nature abhors a vacuum. If this vacuum remains unfilled, your unconscious will automatically refer to and go back to what it knows—your old ways of thinking, feeling, and acting. Instead, to empower yourself for greater confidence and success, you want to fill this vacuum with positive, new, and empowering ways of thinking, feeling and acting. That is the focus of this and the next three chapters.

Keeping a commitment to yourself

When you make a decision, a resolution or tell yourself that you will do or change something, you are essentially making a commitment to yourself. Yet, year after year many people continue to let themselves down. Why? Because the two essential ingredients for keeping any commitment to yourself are missing. Firstly, you need to have absolute clarity about what it is that you want, combined with absolute certainty that you can achieve it. Secondly, you need to know why you want it—you need to have a compelling purpose for doing it.

7.2   Purpose and Goals

The power of purpose

We all have a higher purpose in life—a purpose that extends beyond the physical, mental, and emotional realms. To become aware of our true purpose in life, we need to allow ourselves to be completely open and vulnerable to our true selves. And we can only do that once we stop judging ourselves, putting ourselves down, and beating up on ourselves. It begins with total appreciation, gratitude, and love of our true self.

Once we discover our life purpose and set goals that are aligned with that purpose, we will find more passion, drive, confidence, and success in life. Then, every action we take towards achieving our goals will seem effortless and enjoyable. The techniques in this book will empower you to begin this journey.

Always have a purpose—a compelling "why" you want to achieve something—as it will motivate you and help you to more easily achieve it. So let's begin with baby steps. Below please write down one task that you have been putting off or delaying completing which, once you action it, will improve your life. Go with the first task that comes to mind (e.g. update my résumé, open a savings account).

_____

_____

Next, write down what is *the one action* you can take right now towards the above task, e.g. send an email, make a call, or do research.

_____

_____

Then write down a realistic timeframe for taking action on the above step.

_____

_____

Now think about the cost to you (in time, money, emotions, and energy) of *not* doing this task?

_____

_____

_____

_____

Next, write down *all the benefits to you* of completing this task. Why do you want to do this task? What will this task help you to be, do, have, and achieve?

_____

_____

_____

_____

_____

_____

_____

_____

Next, visualise this task turning out successfully—this will stop any worry, dread, or anxiety about doing the task. Below are the steps to assist you with this:

1. Be clear about your outcome for that task. What specifically would you like to achieve (e.g. complete one hour of research)?
2. With your eyes closed, think about the above task you have chosen—where, when, and with whom will you be when you are doing it?
3. Imagine a movie screen in front of you and see yourself in the movie like an actor or actress completing that task at the date and location you choose to do the task.
4. As you watch the movie, see yourself successfully com-

pleting that task, hear the conversations you would like to hear, feel exactly how you would like to feel, and make sure your self-talk is positive as you do that task. Make sure you focus on what is within your control and the task turning out 100% successfully, and how you easily achieve your outcome for that task.

5. Notice how you now feel about that task when you focus on what you want, and how you now look forward to it. Open your eyes feeling confident and motivated about doing that task.

Now it is time to carry out this task—that's right, just allocate the time to do this task, then do it. You can even use your resource anchor (Chapter 5) to feel positive emotions before and while doing that task. Enjoy taking the action and notice how you feel once it is completed. Then repeat the above steps separately for any other tasks you wish to complete. For tasks involving many steps or longer timeframes, I suggest you set specific goals for those using the steps below.

Creating your life

While there are uncertainties around you, things out of your control—you can make your life more certain for yourself. The more certain you are about your future, the more confident you will feel about it.

Creating your life begins with you thinking about what you really want. The process below will help you really clarify what you want. Simply answer the seven questions below and notice the end result. The example in brackets will assist you in case you need some help with this. Allow yourself about fifteen minutes to effectively complete this before proceeding.

1. List below all the areas in your life (e.g. health, finances, family, relationships, friends, career or business, personal development).

_____

_____

_____

_____

_____

_____

_____

_____

2. As you think about the next 12 months, which *one* of the above areas of life is your top priority to focus on, improve, or make more successful? Write this below (e.g. career).

_____

3. What specifically would you like to achieve *for yourself* in this area of your life in the next 12 months? (e.g. get a promotion, mainly for me, even though others will benefit indirectly from my goal). Write this below.

_____

_____

_____

_____

4. By when do you want to achieve this? Which date?
   (e.g. realistically, by my next performance review in July
   next year).

_____

_____

5. What skills, qualities, resources, and other people's support do you have now that will help you to achieve this?
   (e.g. I have the qualifications I need to do that job, I
   have the confidence and self-belief, and I have a good
   relationship with my manager).

_____

_____

_____

_____

6. What other skills, qualities, resources, and other people's
   support do you need to learn or source to help you to
   achieve this? (e.g. I need to further develop my communication and influencing skills, as I will be dealing with

many people within the organisation at different levels. I need my manager's support. I need to demonstrate to her that I am competent to be promoted and can do that job well.)

_____

_____

_____

_____

7. Is what you want to achieve safe, legal, moral, and ethical for all (you, your family, friends, society, and the environment)? (E.g. Yes, everyone will ultimately benefit in a positive way from me achieving this.)

_____

_____

_____

_____

SMART goal setting

Next, let's turn this want into a specific goal so it is more achievable for you. We will use the SMART principles below to help you to make your goals far more achievable. My version of SMART is:

- Short, simple sentence
- Makes sense
- Achievable
- Resilient mindset
- Time to action it

A short, simple sentence

Make sure that your goal is a short and simple sentence. Write your goal out in a single sentence, specifically stating what you want. Avoid vague goals like "get a promotion," "lose weight," or "make more money." Also avoid saying things like, "I want to lose x kilos." Instead of saying what you want to lose, say what you want to achieve, e.g. "I weigh 70 kg." My experience has been that people who set goals to lose weight usually put on weight.

Makes sense

A goal will make sense if you can measure it, and if it is safe and responsible. The only way you will know that you have successfully achieved your goal is if you have a way of measuring it. How will you measure the success of your goal? For example, standing on the scales and seeing the target weight, fitting into smaller-size pants, or some other way? Or receiving a letter confirming your promotion, seeing your new payslip, or an email announcing your promotion to the team?

Achievable

Make sure that your goal is achievable and realistic within the timeframe you set. Avoid setting yourself up to not achieve your goals by having an unreasonable deadline or where you expect yourself to do things outside your skill level. Some skills take time to learn, so allow yourself time to learn these. Make the timeframe for your goals realistic and hence achievable. Always set yourself up for success while at the same time challenging yourself to grow.

You want to set both long-term and short-term goals to stay motivated. Long-term goals keep us motivated to achieve short-term goals. For example, setting a long-term goal of owning your own home will help you to stay motivated to save for a home deposit in the short-term. Without the long-term goal, it is easier to give up on the short-term goal, to get off track and be distracted by instant and fun activities instead (e.g. shopping for clothes, or going out). On the other hand, if you only have long-term goals without short-term goals, you may get overwhelmed by the enormity of the goal and stop taking action. Having short-term goals (baby steps towards achieving our long-term goals) is the key to taking action and staying focused.

To ensure your goal is achievable and realistic, below write down the key actions you need to take to achieve it. Next to each one, note the date by when you will complete each of these steps.

Action	Date

Action	Date

Resilient mindset

This means that you have the mental fortitude to achieve your goals despite any challenges. Ensure you fully believe in your ability to achieve your goals and also in your ability to bounce back quickly after any challenge. This is how highly successful people achieve their goals—persistence and having mental buoyancy to bounce back fast are key. Ensure that all negative emotions, limiting beliefs, and internal conflicts about your ability to achieve your goal and to bounce back after a challenge are fully addressed, as we have already discussed in the previous chapters. This will ensure you have the confidence to easily achieve your goals.

Time to action it

Many people state what they want without a timeframe, e.g. one day I will reach my goal weight or get a promotion. This makes the goal difficult to achieve, as your mind needs a target date to work towards. Pick a specific date by when you want to achieve your goal and make sure the date is realistic and safe. For a health goal, avoid setting a goal to reduce weight by ten kilos in one week—this is both unsafe and unsustainable long-term. Likewise, if you need time to learn a skill, make sure this is reflected in the date of your goal.

Also make sure that your goal is written in the present tense (e.g. I am, I now...) rather than the future tense (I will, I want to). Goals stated in the future tense never come; they remain in the future and are harder to achieve.

Your SMART goal

Keeping in mind all the SMART criteria above, now write out your goal below. For example, "It is 30 November 2014 and I now weigh seventy kilos." Or, "It is now 31 July 2015 and I secure the promotion to manager of operations at [name of company]." Notice that these goals are specific about date and weight or job role, they are a short simple sentence, they make sense, and they are written in the present tense. We will assume that **the goals are achievable** and that the person setting the goal has a resilient mindset.

My SMART goal:

_____

_____

Once you are happy with your goal, it is time to program your unconscious to help you to more easily achieve it. Simply follow the steps below.

1. Remember where your resource anchor is (please refer to Chapter 5).
2. With your eyes closed, imagine a movie screen in front of you.
3. See yourself in the movie like an actor or actress at a future date, seeing yourself in the movie achieving your goal.
4. Make sure you have a picture of yourself in the movie, along with any sounds, feelings, self-talk, tastes, and smells associated with achieving your goal.
5. Intensify all of these senses and the self-talk as you watch yourself in the movie, achieving your goal, and really feel how that feels.
6. Feel the emotions you feel as you watch yourself in the movie. Notice the positive images, sounds, feelings, tastes, smells and self-talk around achieving your goal.
7. Anchor that positive feeling in your resource anchor.
8. Open your eyes feeling confident about taking action to achieve your goal.

You can repeat the seven questions from the section "Creating your life" in this chapter to clarify what you want to achieve in the other areas of your life, then turn them into SMART goals and visualise them. Then take action towards these and enjoy the journey!

Reward yourself

Rewards are a great way to celebrate our successes, achievements, and victories. It is important to reward yourself when you achieve your goals. Goals take energy and effort, and your unconscious likes to be rewarded when it helps you to achieve success. Some examples could include: the latest technology or fashion items, a car, a holiday, day trips, massages, adventures, or movies.

As you think about the SMART goal you wrote above, choose a reward for yourself now, making sure it is a sufficient reward for your goal. For example, if your goal is small, choose a small reward. Choose a large reward for a large goal. Importantly, make sure you reward yourself once you achieve your goal, and enjoy the celebration!

My reward:

_____

_____

7.3   *Creating certainty*

Setting and achieving goals is a great way to create certainty for yourself and your life. Achieving goals also builds your confidence and success. In addition to setting and achieving goals, other ways for you to create a certain and confident future include:

1. **Develop inner certainty.** Address negative emotions, limiting beliefs, and internal conflicts as discussed in previous chapters. Make sure you fully address these. They are the greatest causes of uncertainty and saboteurs of confidence and success, as they have us question ourselves and the future.

2. **Only think about what you want.** Use empowering and positive language, and avoid disempowering language (refer to Chapter 6). Use the process for banishing anxiety (Chapter 5). Remember, whether you think about what you want or what you don't want, it will become self-fulfilling through your thoughts, emotions, and behaviour.

3. **Take action.** In the absence of action, you will feel like you are treading water—at a standstill—neither moving forward nor backwards. Action creates momentum and helps you to move towards what you want. We discuss this in detail in Chapter 10.

4. **Calmly does it.** To create a certainty of calm and manage your emotions, remember to use the instant calm technique from Chapter 6.

5. **Instant confidence and success.** To ensure you feel confidence whenever you wish to, remember to use your confidence anchor. To feel four or five positive emotions at the same time, use your resource anchor. Please refer to Chapter 5 for details.

6. **Let go.** Let go of having to have your goals and what you want. Letting go gives you certainty. This requires trust in yourself and your ability to achieve it. Address any negative emotions, limiting beliefs, and inner conflicts that prevent you from fully trusting yourself.

7. **Celebrate and refocus.** Once you achieve one goal, celebrate. Then refocus and set your next goal. Goals provide you with motivation and your motivation levels may decrease if you stop setting more goals. Achieving goals boosts your confidence and also helps you to achieve greater success, which in turn, increases your confidence

further.

8. **Create a Supportive Environment**. Choose people and situations that support and empower you rather than disempower you. This includes who you surround yourself with at work and socially, and what you watch, listen to, and read. Chapter 9 discusses this in detail.

When you let go of what you want, it is far easier to achieve it. Think of your goal like a boomerang—when you let it go and throw it out into the distance, only then does it come back to you. However, if you hold onto your goal (or the boomerang) with the desperation of having to have it, it will never come back to you and will be harder to achieve.

How we relate to other people, both personally and professionally, also affects our confidence and success. The next chapter explains simple and effective communication techniques to help you be more confident and successful in your personal and professional relationships.

7.4   Summary

The key messages that we covered in this chapter include:

- You already know what you want and have all the answers that you seek inside of you right now.
- Always have a purpose for taking any action, for doing anything in life; it will motivate you and help you to more easily achieve it.
- Make your life more certain. With certainty comes confidence. Begin by thinking about what you really want and turning your wants into SMART goals.

- Let go of having to have your goals and what you want. Letting go requires trust in yourself and gives you certainty.
- Achieving goals boosts your confidence and also helps you to achieve greater success, which in turn increases your confidence further.

7.5   Your action journey

What action will you now take after having read this chapter? Please note your action items from this chapter in your practice plan in Chapter 10 of this book.

8. Building your competence

Confident and competent communication

When we all think alike, no one thinks very much.

—Albert Einstein

In previous chapters of this book, we discussed techniques to assist you with increasing your confidence and your success. It is important to complement strong levels of confidence with competence—the skills for success.

To create harmonious personal and professional relationships, it is important to address any negative emotions, limiting beliefs, and internal conflicts around communicating and interacting with people. The previous chapters will have assisted you with this. If we feel confident within ourselves, yet how we communicate with others causes conflict or disagreements, the latter could compromise our levels of confidence.

8.1   *Effective communication is the key*

Good communication skills are a key set of skills that will serve you well for life, both personally and professionally. Because we communicate with people every day, knowing how to consistently and clearly get our message through will reduce disagreements, conflicts, and misunderstandings. By facilitating harmonious personal and professional relationships through your communication, you will build your confidence further.

Your communication is powerful, and it has the potential to build trust and create close relationships or to cause schisms and conflict. If your requests and suggestions fall on deaf ears, after a while this can undermine your confidence in yourself and in dealing with people. Ultimately, this can negatively impact on your personal and professional relationships. How you communicate will either influence others to work towards achieving win-win outcomes or not. That is the focus of this chapter—how to communicate effectively to achieve win-win outcomes, both personally and professionally.

Principles of effective communication

Let's begin by understanding the five key NLP-based principles for effective communication.

Principle 1—The map is different to the territory

As discussed in Chapter 2, every second we are inundated by around 2 million bits of information—we call this "the territory." Our brain can only process around 126 bits per second—we call this "the map." So we only ever have a map of the territory: our own version of what has happened at an event or what was said. For example, your recollection of what was discussed or what happened during a meeting or a family gathering may be quite different to that of your colleagues and your siblings.

Often people disagree and argue over these events, insisting that their "map" (interpretation or recollection) of "the territory" (an event) is correct and other people's "maps" are incorrect. Instead of arguing over who is right or wrong, it is more effective to realise that your map is different to other people's maps. To understand others' maps and how they interpret situations, you need to understand their values, beliefs, and other filters, which we mentioned in Chapter 2.

Principle 2—Respect different models of the world

Because each person has their own map of a situation based on their filters, we respect those differences. We never say that one person's view is right and another's is wrong, or judge their views: we respect the different points of view.

This is similar to Einstein's general theory of relativity, which says that no observer (and their frame of reference) is special. Relativity says that everybody is equal and your point of view or your vantage point as an observer is as valid as mine. There isn't a preferred frame of reference or vantage point; they are only different frames of reference.

By respecting another person's view of the world, we step into it for the purpose of understanding it, all the while remaining true to our own values, beliefs, and view of the world.

Rather than forcing others to change their model of the world to fit into ours, we learn how to communicate effectively with people who hold different views of the world. When we appreciate another person's viewpoint, it is easier for us to understand them, to relate to them, and to be more effective in our communication with them.

Principle 3—Flexibility achieves outcomes

Following on from the first two principles above, Principle 3 says that the more flexible you are, the more likely it is that you will achieve your outcome. So if your outcome is to clearly communicate your message, this will be much easier once you realise that different people have different views, maps, and models of the world. By better understanding what makes other people "tick," the more effective you will be in communicating with them.

You can apply the communication techniques in this chapter to be more flexible in achieving win-win outcomes. If on the other hand, you continue to only communicate in the same way that you have been to date, you will limit your flexibility in communicating with a range of different personalities. In turn, this could lead to conflict, disagreements, and misunderstandings with some people.

Principle 4—There is never failure, only feedback

The response you receive from other people to your communication is your feedback as to the effectiveness of your communication. Instead of thinking you failed, if how you communicated gave you a negative or undesired response, use that as feedback to adjust your communication. Be flexible, and use feedback to adjust your communication until you succeed.

When relating to other people, frustration is your feedback that you need to do something different to achieve a successful outcome. This is where it is important to communicate in new ways that match the preference of the person you are communicating with.

If you feel frustrated when you communicate with other people, check the following:

- Is the emotion of frustration in proportion to the situation? If so, refer to the second point below. If not, address the emotion of frustration as discussed in previous chapters.

- Are you continuing to communicate in the same ways and you keep getting the same response? If so, be flexible and use the communication skills in this chapter to be flexible next time you communicate with that person.

Remember, frustration is futile. Focus on what is within your control and how you are communicating and influencing other people. Rather than focusing on how other people behave, focus on how you can change your approach to other people.

Principle 5—Resistance is a sign of lack of rapport

Anytime you are communicating with someone and you receive resistance or push back to your message, it is your feedback, a sign to develop stronger rapport with that person.

When people feel they have rapport with you, they feel comfortable to open up to you and are more receptive to your message. Resistance means you have insufficient rapport with them. Later in this chapter, we will discuss how you can easily develop rapport with other people.

While there are many effective communication techniques I could share with you, below you will find several simple techniques to help you improve the effectiveness of your communication quickly.

Stop the dramas

How do you respond when other people question you or have objections to your suggestions? Do you take these too personally, or do you handle them objectively? If you respond to questions and objections emotionally because your "buttons" have been pushed, your message will be lost in the delivery. The other person will be focusing on your anger, frustration, or hurt, rather than on the content of your message. Ensure that you address your "buttons" as discussed in earlier chapters, so that your communication is more effective and your message is really heard by the other person.

A clear outcome

How many times have you left a meeting wondering what you achieved? Perhaps you were frustrated or annoyed that the meeting was a waste of time and had no purpose? Prior to communicating with anyone, think about the desired outcome for your communication. What would you like to achieve?

Before making a phone call, sending an email, or having a meeting, always think about your outcome. When you have an outcome that is clear, your thoughts, words, and actions will be more purposeful and you will be much more effective in achieving your outcome. Also, ensure your outcome is a win-win and will benefit everyone.

For example, your desired outcome for communicating with another person could be any of the following (depending on whether it is a personal or professional situation):

- arrange to go out
- stay in touch and say hello
- understand the other person's needs
- arrange a meeting
- touch base to check if they need any help or support
- answer any questions

- follow up on an email or mail-out you sent

As you think about each of the above, notice that the following will be different depending on your desired outcome:

- what you say
- the questions you ask
- what you bring with you
- who you bring with you
- where and how you meet
- your preparation

Below are some questions you can ask yourself to clarify your desired outcome, together with a personal and professional example to assist you.

1. What specifically do I want to achieve from this phone call, email, or meeting?
   - Personal example: I have a fun evening out with my family.
   - Professional example: We agree on the next step for this project.
2. How will I be able to measure that my outcome has been achieved?
   - Personal example: I feel happy and enjoy the conversations with my family.
   - Professional example: At the end of the meeting, we all agree on the next step and the timeframe, and allocate responsibilities to achieving these.
3. What are the key steps I and other people need to take to achieve this outcome?
   - Personal example: I bring my camera to take some photos of the evening.

- Professional example: I bring my laptop or iPad and project status reports to help us make a decision on the next step, and ask other attendees to do the same.

Think about the next time you will communicate with someone (in person, on the phone, or via email) and clarify your desired outcome beforehand by answering the questions below:

What specifically do I want to achieve from this phone call, email, or meeting?

\
\

How will I be able to measure that my outcome has been achieved?

\
\

What are the key steps I and other people need to take to achieve this outcome?

\
\

Visualise success

Once you are clear about your outcome, to take the worry, anxiety, and dread out of the communication, mentally rehearse successfully achieving the desired outcome in advance. Whether you worry about or dread a negative communication, or you look forward to a positive outcome, what you expect will become self-fulfilling through your thoughts, feelings, and actions, as discussed in previous chapters. Simply follow the steps in the "Banish anxiety" section of Chapter 5 to visualise a successful outcome.

The right state

Ensure you are in the right state during your communication by using the techniques discussed in Chapter 5.

1. Use "instant calm" for calm, rather than stressful, communication. If you are calm during your conversation, the other person will be too. If you are stressed, the other person will be too; they will pick up on your state, especially when you have a strong rapport with them.
2. Use "instant confidence" to feel confident during your communication. Simply use your confidence anchor.
3. Use your resource anchor to feel a combination of positive emotions at the same time and be in a resourceful state.
4. Let go of emotions about recent events so you avoid being consumed by them and you are more objective during your communication.

8.2   *Developing rapport*

Resistance or warm reception?

Do you sometimes feel that your communication flows easily and at other times it is like pulling teeth? Would you like to stop facing resistance to your ideas and suggestions and get a warm reception instead?

A natural flow

When there is a natural flow between people, they feel totally comfortable expressing their opinions and views with each other, however different those views may be. They freely discuss problems, ideas, solutions, and challenges, and feel at ease with each other as they do so. Sometimes family members, friends, partners, and colleagues can get out of this natural flow with each other. This often occurs when too many negative associations or disagreements occur between them over a period of time. Unconsciously, they link negatives to each other, and the flow they once felt is there less often or may even disappear after a while.

Instant rapport

If you feel there is a lack of connection—that the natural flow is missing—between you and your family member, friend, partner, colleague, or manager, it is important to establish rapport with them prior to your communication. You may wish to have a separate outcome to first get into rapport with the person you wish to communicate with so that you can more easily achieve your desired outcome for communicating with them.

When you are in rapport with other people, there is a greater trust and connection between you. Any ideas or suggestions you make, even if they are different to the other person's, will at least be more easily considered when you have rapport with them. While they may still disagree with you, at least with rapport they will hear you out and consider your perspective, rather than automatically dismissing it or cutting you off.

Getting into rapport

There are several different ways to get into rapport with another person, both personally and professionally. When you are face to face with another person, the best way to get into rapport is to match or mirror their physiology. When you do this, it is important to be subtle so that it remains out of the other person's conscious awareness.

While there are many different ways of getting into rapport with other people, a simple and the fastest way to get into rapport is to match the other person's breathing. Watch and discretely match the location of their breathing (i.e. high chest, mid chest, or stomach) and/or the rate of their breathing (i.e. fast, medium, or slow). Slow down or speed up your rate of breathing to match theirs. Also, shift the location of your breathing by changing your physiology. An upright physiology helps you breathe from high in your chest, while a laid-back posture helps you breathe from your stomach.

Within minutes of matching the other person's breathing, you will feel a warm feeling of comfort around your stomach area, like an "at home" feeling with them. When you are feeling comfortable with them, they are also feeling comfortable with you—you are both in rapport with each other. They will then feel more comfortable to open up and share problems and ideas with you and will be more receptive to your ideas and hearing you out. Instead of resistance, you will get a warm reception from them. Notice how with greater rapport your personal and professional relationships become even stronger.

Communicating with different styles

There are four different communication styles, and we all use a combination of all four. While we have a preference for one or two styles over the rest, so do our family members, friends, partner, colleagues, and manager. This is why it is important to understand any similarities and differences. When our communication preferences are different to those around us, misunderstandings and disagreements can occur. By understanding your own and other people's styles, and being aware of any differences, you can avoid frustration and disagreements with them.

Below you will find the four different styles, together with tips to assist you to be more effective in communicating with each style. This is another great way to build rapport with other people as you communicate with them. As you read through each style, notice which one(s) reflect your current preference and which reflect your least preferred style(s) right now. Please be aware that your preferences, and other people's, can change from time to time.

The thinker

The thinker likes to analyse, compare, and think through things. They like facts and figures, data, research, statistics, and proof. Things need to be logical and make sense to the thinker.

To communicate effectively with a person of this preference, use words like:

- think
- understand
- consider
- analyse
- study
- decide

This will help them make sense out of what you say. Avoid being vague. Be specific, get to the point, and ensure your argument is logical; otherwise, what you say may not make sense to them.

The feeler

The feeler experiences life mainly through their emotions. They like hugs and touch. Because they are very hands-on, they like to do and experience things rather than just being told how they work. To communicate effectively with a person of this preference, use words like:

- feel
- touch
- hold
- connect
- calm
- solid

This will help them get a grasp of what you say. Avoid coming across as unfeeling by talking about processes and steps, or they may not feel a connection with you.

The talker

The talker likes to talk about problems and experiences, and loves speaking on the phone and/or face to face. They are attuned to sounds and can be easily distracted. To communicate effectively with someone of this preference, use words like:

- talk
- sounds
- discuss
- listen
- rings a bell
- loud

This will help them hear what you say. Avoid showing them maps or directions; instead, give them verbal instructions and directions so that they can more easily follow along.

The looker

The looker likes to see things, diagrams, drawings, and pictures. They are good at imagining things and being creative. Their environment and their own appearance is important to them. To communicate effectively with someone of this preference, use words like:

- look
- show
- imagine
- view

- clear
- perspective

This will help them see what you are saying. Avoid too many verbal instructions or directions, as they will get "lost." Instead, show them maps and diagrams that they can see.

Pay attention to the words your family members, friends, partner, colleagues, and manager use, and then use the same words back when you communicate with them. Notice the greater connection and understanding this leads to, and how it strengthens your relationships with them.

8.3   It's in the delivery

When you communicate with people personally or professionally do you come across as commanding or authoritarian? Do you sound credible or unsure? Your tone of voice will send unconscious signals to the listener. While your intent may be to be empathetic, if your tone of voice is authoritarian or commanding, the other person will focus on your tone of voice rather than on the content of your message. Your message will be lost in the delivery. On the other hand, if your tone of voice sounds questioning, you will sound unsure and uncertain and your family, friends, partner, colleagues, and manager will question you more about your ideas and requests.

The best tone of voice to use when making a request or offering a solution is to end your sentences in a level tonality, where your voice avoids fluctuating too high or too low at the end. When you end your sentences flat, you sound more credible and believable. Obviously, you also need to deliver on what you say.

The third degree or being uncaring?

Are you upset by all the questions your partner, family members, friends, colleagues, and manager ask you? Do you sometimes feel like other people are giving you the third degree or are interrogating you? Or perhaps you feel that your family members, partner, friends, colleagues, and manager could be more forthcoming with information?

If you prefer the big picture and dislike too much information, you may find that if someone inundates you with too much detail, you become uncomfortable or bored. On the other hand, if you prefer detail and your partner, family members, friends, colleagues, and manager give you minimal information, you may ask them lots of questions, and even get upset if they are not forthcoming with the detail.

For example, when was the last time you asked your partner, friend, family member, colleague, or manager, "How was your day?" Did they give you a short answer like "fine"? Or did they perhaps give you so much information that you found yourself switching off and not listening to what they said? It is important to realise that some people need a lot of detail before they can proceed with a task or make a decision, so they may ask you lots of questions. On the other hand, some people simply need to be told the big picture and may, therefore, ask very few questions if any.

Avoid thinking that your partner, family members, friends, colleague, or manager:

- are being nosy or giving you the third degree if they ask

you lots of questions

- don't care if they don't ask you enough questions
- are being secretive or keeping things from you if they only give you a one- or two-word answer.

Some people have a natural preference for detail, while others prefer the big picture only. It is simply their way of relating to people and the world around them. Start becoming aware of the differences in your style, and other people's styles, so you give them the appropriate level of information. Below are some questions you can ask to assist you with communicating with people of these different styles.

Too much detail

To effectively communicate with a person who is caught up in too much detail and who is asking you too many questions, ask them these questions to assist them with seeing the big picture:

- "What is your intention...?" e.g. What is your intention for going on this holiday?
- "What is your objective...?"
- "What is your desired outcome...?"

These questions will bring them out of the detail and help them to "see the forest from the trees." Asking these questions will also assist you to reach win-win agreements with them, and help them with making decisions.

Tell me more

To effectively communicate with a person who is only giving you one- or two-word answers when you want more information, ask them these questions:

- "What, specifically...?" e.g. What, specifically, would you like to do?
- "Who, specifically...?
- "How, specifically...?"

Asking these questions will help them access more information and give you more detail. Of course, you also want to respect their style and avoid asking too many questions, or they may feel that you are being too nosy even if that is not your intention.

By being aware of the differences between your style and other people's styles, you can use the above communication techniques to easily and effectively create happier, more fulfilling, and successful personal and professional relationships.

Beware the comfort zone

You have your own natural preferences in how you communicate with other people. Beware of staying in your comfort zone and only using your natural preference in communicating with other people if their preference is different to yours. This is a sure-fire way to disengage others, which can result in disagreements and arguments and can negatively affect your confidence. It is a common challenge I come across when working with couples to improve their relationships and in working with business people in creating harmonious teams.

By being flexible and developing your competence in your communication, you will more easily develop harmonious and fulfilling personal and professional relationships. In turn, this will further build your confidence and success.

Stepping out of your comfort zone may also mean ensuring you support yourself for ongoing confidence and success. The next chapter focuses on how to create a supportive and empowering environment to help you do this.

8.4   Summary

The key messages that we covered in this chapter include:

- The response you receive from other people to your communication is your feedback as to the effectiveness of your communication.
- Once you are clear about your desired outcome, mentally rehearse a successful outcome in advance, and ensure you are in the right state during your communication.
- When you are in rapport with other people, your views and ideas will be heard rather than being automatically dismissed.
- Pay attention to the words other people use and the amount of information they need, and then be flexible in your communication so you build harmonious and successful relationships with them.
- Staying in your comfort zone when communicating could lead to disagreements and arguments, which could negatively affect your confidence.

8.5   *Your action journey*

What action will you now take after having read this chapter? Please note your action items from this chapter in your practice plan in Chapter 10 of this book.

9. Supporting yourself for success

Creating an empowering environment

Great spirits have always encountered violent opposition from mediocre minds.

—Albert Einstein

Now that you have learned some techniques to empower yourself for greater confidence, competence, and success, it is critical to nurture that investment in yourself. Often this means ensuring that your environment supports your success. How to manage your environment for ongoing strong levels of confidence and success is the focus of this chapter.

As discussed in Chapter 1, you can only control how you think, feel, and act, and how you influence people around you. If you are unhappy with other people's behaviour, you can only change how you respond to their behaviour. How we relate to other people's behaviour is very important. This is a huge topic in itself and one that I thoroughly researched as part of my PhD thesis. Please refer to the Appendix for details.

First, you need to identify if you are encouraging an empowering or disempowering dynamic between you and other people. Your dynamic with other people can impact on your levels of confidence and success. For example, if you are part of a supportive culture and a positive dynamic at work, you will probably feel more confident in asking for help and support when you need it. In turn, this will assist you with being more successful. Alternatively, if there is a negative culture and dynamic at work, you may avoid speaking with people or asking for help, which could have you feel isolated and unsupported. This could negatively impact on your confidence, performance and success.

Research has shown that toxic employees have significant detrimental impacts on their colleagues. Some of these include angry, frustrated, and dissatisfied employees whose performance decreases or who end up resigning as a result of toxic employees' behaviour. According to a 2009 study, of those employees who choose to stay:

- 66% decreased their performance at work as a result of the negative environment
- 80% lost time worrying about the negative incident(s)
- 63% wasted time avoiding the toxic co-worker or manager

9.1   Transforming disempowering dynamics

Do you feel you are "between a rock and hard place" and whatever you do, your partner, friends, family members, colleagues, or manager aren't happy? Are you frustrated or upset by the games other people play?

The catch-22

Any time you feel that you are being backed into a corner as a result of your partner, friend, family member, colleague, or manager saying or doing something, you are caught in a catch-

22. You can't win either way—whether you do or don't do what they ask, you are made out to be wrong for it. Below are a few common examples to assist you with identifying any catch-22s in your personal and professional relationships.

Partner games

Partner A says, "If you loved me, you would know what to do." Partner B does not know what partner A needs, so they do what they think they need, and are reprimanded by partner A for getting it wrong. Partners are not mind readers. Instead, each partner needs to share what they need in a relationship and then meet each other's needs in empowering ways.

Partner C says, "Why can't you be spontaneous and arrange a romantic dinner?" Then when partner D does arrange the romantic dinner, partner C replies, "You only did that because I told you to." Partner D is in a no-win situation.

Family and friend games

Sibling E is upset when sibling F is spoilt by their parents and she is not. Then when the parents go to give attention and support, and spoil sibling E, she refuses it. The parents are in a no-win situation.

Friend G wants to stop smoking and has asked friend H to help him to stop buying cigarettes. Friend H has agreed to support him. When friend H goes shopping, friend G insists that friend H buys him cigarettes. If friend H refuses in order to help him give up that habit, friend G gets angry with him. Friend H is made out to be wrong for supporting friend G.

Work games

Colleague K says to colleague L, "Why do you let her push you around? You should stand up to her." Then when colleague L stands up for herself, colleague K, who told her to do so, makes colleague L out to be wrong for doing so, because it upset their mutual manager. Instead, colleague K should be supportive of colleague L.

A manager offers to help an employee with any challenges on a project. Then when the employee seeks help from the manager, the manager gets upset about being asked for help. The employee was simply responding to the manager's offer of help.

Ending the games

Often these games occur on an unconscious level, without you or other people being aware of the dynamic. The first step is awareness. Become aware of any games you may be playing with your partner, friends, family members, colleagues, or manager. Once these are identified, then you need to stop the games. The best way to stop the games is to address any negative emotions, limiting beliefs, and internal conflicts that each of you have so that the dynamic between you changes. We discussed how you can do this in earlier chapters.

Because you are unable to change other people's behaviour or force them to make changes that they are unhappy to make, the best you can do is to address your own patterns of sabotage that are contributing to the disempowering dynamic. Also, if your loved ones, colleagues, and manager are open to changing their behaviour, you could respectfully and politely suggest to them to get some support or to read this book so it can also assist them with making changes in their behaviour.

An important distinction

Rather than labelling your partner, friend, family member, colleague, or manager as bad or mean because of their behaviour and the games they play on an unconscious level, realise that they are doing the best they can with what they have learned, what they know and how they were brought up. They are probably unaware of these unconscious games, just as you may have been unaware of them until now.

People are much more than their behaviour. Distinguish between them as people and their behaviour. See everybody in your life as wonderful human beings and only describe their behaviour as less than wonderful.

Keep this in mind when communicating with them. Instead of saying, "I don't like you when you say, 'If you loved me, you would know what to do,'" you could say "You know I like/love you, it is just some of your behaviour I dislike. For example, when you (insert behaviour)..."

Never put the other person down or make them out to be wrong for their behaviour. Only refer to their behaviour and how you would like their behaviour to change towards you.

Remember this rule of thumb—if you can't say something nice, don't say anything at all. Once words are spoken, you can never take them back.

Sibling rivalry

Are you overly competitive with your brothers or sisters? Do you go into a jealous rage when your siblings excel, succeed, or perform better than you?

Sibling rivalry is another potentially disempowering dynamic. It is competition between siblings for love and attention from parents and other relatives. When siblings are growing up, they can compete for their parents' love, affection, and attention, and they can be sensitive to differences in parental treatment from a very early age.

When children feel they are getting unequal amounts of their parents' attention, fighting between siblings can occur. This rivalry can continue into adulthood with competition for who is the most successful, most acknowledged, or most accomplished in the family. While healthy competition between siblings can help each to excel and succeed, unhealthy competition can be very disempowering and damaging.

Insecurities feed the rivalry

Unhealthy sibling rivalry can only exist if siblings have their own insecurities, because it is those insecurities that feed the rivalry through emotions such as jealousy, envy, resentment, betrayal, anger, and limiting beliefs. Rivalry can develop very early on in life, based on how each sibling interprets their upbringing and their relationship with their parents.

It can take only one event in early childhood to trigger sibling rivalry. For example, a new brother or sister being born can cause the existing sibling to feel jealous, abandoned, or unloved as a result of more attention being given to the newborn. With those emotions left unaddressed, subsequent family dynamics can be misinterpreted by that sibling in a negative way, adding to those emotions and fuelling the sibling rivalry.

Family dynamics

The order of birth (firstborn, middle child, youngest), and being compared to other siblings, can also create rivalry that can continue into adulthood. Think of the TV show *Everybody Loves Raymond*, where Raymond is the youngest, spoiled son, while Robert, the eldest son, feels unloved. The two brothers constantly compete for their mother's attention and recognition, and the mother encourages and thrives on it.

Innocent, off-the-cuff comments parents make (e.g. "Why can't you be like your sister?") can be interpreted by a child as them being judged, not being good enough, or being unloved. Too much attention directed at one child, or more support for one child and their hobbies than another, can create the perception of favouritism. Differences in how school and sporting achievements are acknowledged and compared between siblings can also create such perceptions. Extra hugs or comments by relatives directed at one sibling over another sibling can create rivalry, unhealthy competition, perfectionist behaviours, and more.

Even significant emotional events in adulthood can trigger childhood memories long forgotten, or unconscious rivalries between siblings. For example, two brothers had a very harmonious relationship with each other until one brother went through a very bitter divorce, which brought up his insecurities from childhood about being unloved. This revealed a subtle unconscious rivalry between the two brothers that existed since childhood, and started an outright competition between the two over whose children were more accomplished.

Ending the rivalry

As you reflect on your relationship with your siblings, notice your response to them, and how your parents and relatives treat you and your brothers and sisters. Do you constantly think about how to outdo your sibling (for example, going on and on about your successes, compared to your brother's or sister's achievements, at family events)?

Once you have identified your unhealthy patterns, commit to ending the cycle. Refer to Chapters 3 to 8 in this book to assist you with this. To the extent that you still hold onto past hurts, you will keep having these "buttons" pushed by your siblings and family until you resolve them. Similarly, if you have limiting beliefs around being judged, being unloved, and so on, and if these are left unresolved, they can also trigger an overreaction to what your siblings and family say or do, and lead to rivalry.

9.2   Need versus want

Some people get into a relationship or a new career because they feel they need to be in a relationship or they need to have a career. The relationship or career gives them a sense of completeness, fulfils what is missing inside of them, or meets the social expectations or obligations they feel upon them. Other people enter a relationship or career already feeling complete within themselves. The relationship or career adds to their happiness, and they want to share their happiness with other people. Rather than out of desperation, need, or obligation, they enter a relationship or career because they want one.

People who are needy will generally do anything and put up with anything just to get love, attention, and acceptance. This is because their neediness is driven by limiting beliefs such as "I don't deserve to be loved" or "I am not worthy of a relationship," for example. It is beliefs such as these that will affect how they think and feel about themselves, and how they behave in a relationship or career. The neediest of people will compromise themselves for love and attention.

Push-pull

When we enter any personal or professional relationship, a dynamic forms between two or more people where each person can pick up and sense the other person's energy. When one person enters a relationship out of desperation or neediness, it affects how they think, what they say, and how they behave. For example, a needy partner, A, may want to spend all their spare time with the other partner, B, while B may want some time for him or herself. If partner B feels suffocated by partner A's neediness and demands for love and attention, partner B may pull away.

The more the needy partner A "pushes" their neediness on partner B, the more partner B will "pull" away from partner A. The needy partner A in turn feels that the love and attention they need is even more lacking, so they "push" even more to have this need met. Partner B responds by "pulling" further away. This dynamic can continue until one or both partners get frustrated, which may result in a disagreement, an argument, or even a break-up.

Why a relationship/career?

Are you currently in a relationship or career because you want one or need one? Or are you seeking a new relationship or career out of want or need? Here is a quick exercise to help you identify your reasons for being in a relationship or having a career. Think about and honestly complete the appropriate sentence below. For each option A and B, choose either 1 or 2—whichever is most relevant to your current circumstances.

Option A: Relationship

1. I am seeking a new relationship because...
2. I am seeking to stay in my current relationship because...

Option B: Career

1. I am seeking a new career because...
2. I am seeking to stay in my current career because...

_____

_____

_____

_____

_____

_____

_____

_____

_____

Read through your responses and notice the language you have used. Your language is important as it reflects your beliefs, as well as your motivation for a relationship or career. Words like:

- **can, will, want to, am**: are empowering and expand your options and choices
- **can't, should, have to, need to, must**: are disempowering and limit your choices

Someone in a relationship who consistently says, "I have to be in this relationship," is saying that they have little or no choice except to stay in that relationship. Their language reflects their beliefs around relationships, e.g. "I am expected to be in a relationship by this age" or "all my friends have relationships, so I must have one" or "If I am not in a relationship, I am unlovable/unworthy/don't belong," and so on.

Whether you are currently in a relationship or career or are seeking one, be aware of the dynamic that you are creating through your thoughts, feelings, words, and behaviour. If you are seeking a new relationship, is the dynamic on your dates empowering both you and the other person? If you are currently in a relationship, is the dynamic empowering or disempowering both you and your partner?

If the dynamic is empowering and both of you are truly happy, well done. If not, identify and address the negative emotions, limiting beliefs, and internal conflicts that are contributing to the dynamic (see Chapters 3 to 6) so that you can create a more empowering dynamic on your dates or in your relationship from now on. Do likewise in your career, your job interviews, and your interactions with your colleagues and manager.

9.3   *Create a supportive environment*

Your environment will either help to boost your confidence and success or disempower you. Be careful who you surround yourself with. Choose people who support you and empower you in return.

The science of epigenetics explains how mechanisms other than changes in the underlying DNA sequence (e.g. our environment and our life experiences) affect our genetic activity. The cells that make up our whole mind-body are influenced by our environment, so we need to choose our environmental influences carefully.

Sometimes we will have negative people around us. Our family, friends, partner, colleagues, and manager may be negative and "rain on our parade," criticise our work or suggestions, and be unsupportive. This behaviour is a reflection of their own self-doubts and insecurities, so avoid taking their negativity on-board.

There are at least two ways to deal with negative people and to keep yourself positive:

1. You can leave the negative environment and put yourself in a more positive environment. For example, you could stop seeing your negative friends, see less of your negative relatives, change your partner, or change jobs. However, if on an unconscious level you are sending negative signals in the form of negative emotions, limiting beliefs, and internal conflicts, you will keep attracting negativity in new friends, partners, and colleagues until you address the negativity within you. This is because like attracts like.

2. You can choose to respond differently to the negativity of those around you. While you may be unable to change your family, for example, you can choose how you respond in that environment—how you think, feel, and act around them. While there are many different ways to deal with negative people, below are some simple strategies to assist you.

Be clear about what you want

Without a direction and goals to motivate us, we can be more easily distracted by other people's negativity and demands. Have a clear direction for your life, with specific goals that support the achievement of your dreams, as we discussed in Chapter 7. Make sure that your goals truly inspire and motivate you. With a compelling direction and goals, any negativity from others is less likely to affect you.

Also, be careful who you share your dreams and goals with. Some family members, friends, partners, colleagues, and managers may feel "threatened" by your dreams and goals because of their own insecurities (as discussed in Chapter 4) or lack of direction, and may react negatively to your dreams and goals as a result. Be selective, and share your dreams and goals with those who will support and empower you in achieving them.

Stop accepting negative comments

Every time other people make negative comments, we can choose to take them on-board and start to believe them, or choose to ignore them. If we let the negative comments "slide" without protecting ourselves, we are unconsciously accepting them and taking them on board.

Any negative comments can become limiting beliefs that hold us back. For example, if you hear "this is too hard" over and over again from your partner, family, friends, colleagues, and manager, and if you choose to accept that negative comment, after a while you may find yourself saying the same thing and may even start to believe it. In turn, this may affect your confidence and hold you back from the success you want.

A simple way to protect yourself from taking other people's negative comments on-board is to say to yourself the word "ignore" as you hear the negative comment. This gives your unconscious the suggestion to ignore that comment and prevents you from automatically taking it on-board yourself.

"Help me" or "let me vent"?

Also keep in mind that some of your friends, family members, partner, colleagues, and managers may complain or be negative in response to a challenge that they are facing. Some people like to talk through a challenge with you, with the intention of seeking your help with the challenge. Other people like to talk to you about a challenge with the intent of only venting and having someone listen to them. While they would rather only have a "shoulder to cry on" or someone to listen to them, they may not wish to get help with the challenge.

If so, it is important to respect their wishes and avoid forcing them to solve problems if they are not ready to, as it may lead to disagreements or arguments between you. Instead, check if they would like help. If not, just patiently listen and be there for them without taking on-board the negative comments and problems (as mentioned above). If they are seeking help with a challenge, ask them the best way you can assist them. Again, avoid assuming that your solution is best for them, as this could lead to conflict. This is easy to avoid by simply asking them, "How can I assist you?" or "What is the best way I can help you with this problem?" and empowering them to offer their own solutions.

Also, be careful what you read, watch, and listen to: these potentially negative influences can affect your confidence and success, too. For example, a 2013 study in *Psychological Science* showed that when people were subject to "tough times" messages, it led them to consume 40% more food (out of their need for survival) compared with a control group given neutral messages. So "turning off" negative news can reduce your food consumption and can improve your health. Choose positive influences to further support your confidence and success.

External distractions

Do you get easily distracted by computer games, television, other people's requests, or any other activities? It is fine to have downtime and relax by playing games or watching television, yet if you use them as distractions from taking action on your goals and priorities, this is disempowering you. Because these distractions have you take your focus off your priorities and goals in life, they can sabotage your success. This is why it is so important for you to be clear about your goals and priorities in life, as already discussed. Use the techniques in this book to assist you to stay focused, including:

- Clarify and set your goals—Chapter 7.
- Communicate effectively with people around you, including about your goals and priorities, and when you want time to work on them—Chapter 8.
- Identify and address any negative emotions, limiting beliefs, and internal conflicts that sabotage your goals and communication—Chapters 3 to 6.
- Manage how you think and feel from now on—Chapters 5 and 6.
- Surround yourself with empowering people and environments—Chapter 9 (this chapter).

- Take action on your priorities and goals—Chapter 10.

Making room

Do you make your life so busy that you have no room for what you really want? Is your busy environment a distraction that clutters your mind so you can't focus on what you want? As long as you preoccupy yourself with other things, you will keep yourself from focusing on and having what you really want, thus sabotaging yourself.

If you are in a relationship and you wish to make space for a new more empowering relationship with your current partner, or if you are wanting to attract a new relationship altogether, it is important to create space for the new. The same goes for your career and any other areas of your life. The space you need to create includes the following.

Temporal space

This means making time to nurture your existing relationship and keep the connection and love alive. If you are seeking a new relationship, it means freeing up your time to go out socialising and on dates, and spending time with your new partner. If you are seeking a career change, it means making the time to research and clarify the career you really want, to possibly do further study, to update your résumé, to apply for suitable roles, and to attend interviews and secure the new career. Is there anything preventing you from making the time to take action on what you want?

Environmental space

Have you made space in your life for someone else? For example, do your pets sleep on your bed, leaving no room for a partner? Do you clutter up your environment with projects, old résumés, and information from past jobs, and find your mind cluttered too? If so, declutter your environment and fill that space with love, connection, new job satisfaction, or whatever it is that you really seek.

Freedom from attachments

Are you still holding onto the engagement ring your ex gave you and energetically sending out vibes that you are "engaged"? Are you still upset with your current manager or colleague for what they did years ago, or for what they have not done? Have you let go of attachments and sent the vibe that you are available to deepen your current personal and professional relationships or attract brand new ones?

Head space

Have you let go of past limiting beliefs about personal and professional relationships, e.g. fear of getting hurt, fear of failure, "I can't trust people," fear of being alone, "I'm not worthy"? Do you have clarity about exactly what you do want in these relationships, rather than what you don't want? Have you set specific goals to attract new personal or professional relationships?

Heart space

Have you let go of past anger, hurt, resentment, betrayal, rejection, disappointment, fear, loneliness, and sadness? Is your heart healed and ready for new personal and professional relationships? Have you fully forgiven people so you can put the past behind you and move forward with unconditional love?

Habitual space

Are you too much in your comfort zone and unwilling to change your life to include another person? Too set in your ways and thinking that other people need to change for you? Is your current lifestyle (e.g. partying all night) out of alignment with the relationship, career, or family you really want? Are there any habits (e.g. smoking, drinking, overeating, being messy) that you need to shed to create the confidence and success you really want?

We have discussed how to identify and address the above limitations. If you wish to address any of these limitations so that you can create room for greater confidence and success in your life, make sure you have fully completed the relevant exercises and techniques to help you make your desired changes. Chapter 10 will assist you with prioritising and taking action on these, as well as bringing together all your other insights and learnings from previous chapters so you can easily implement what you have learned and create the ongoing confidence and success you desire.

9.4   *Summary*

The key messages that we covered in this chapter include:

- Your dynamic with other people can positively or negatively impact on your levels of confidence and success.

- Distinguish between the person and their behaviour. The person is wonderful—the behaviour may be less than wonderful.
- Choose people who support you. Your environment will help to boost your confidence and success—or disempower you.
- Distractions can have you take your focus off your priorities and goals in life and therefore sabotage your success.
- It is important to make room for the new so you can create the confidence and success you desire.

9.5   *Your action journey*

What action will you now take after having read this chapter? Please note your action items from this chapter in your practice plan in Chapter 10 of this book.

Phase III

Your practice plan

10. Time for action

The key to maintaining ongoing confidence and success

Genius is one percent inspiration and ninety-nine percent perspiration.

—Thomas Edison, American inventor

Congratulations on your journey so far—you have now reached the point where most people stop and expect things to just happen, without taking any action. Action creates momentum and, like a snowball rolling down the mountain, after a while it builds such momentum that an avalanche occurs. This chapter focuses on how you can implement and practice what you have learned in this book to help you create an avalanche of confidence and success in your life.

Rather than waiting to win the lottery, to receive a windfall, to have someone else do the work for you, or for a magic pill, create your own luck by taking action and making things happen. Avoid expecting things to change without doing anything towards changing them. For example, if you used to stress about money and have stopped doing that as a result of using the techniques in this book, well done. Yet, if you then take no action to create the financial situation you want (e.g. reducing debt, increasing your savings, making more money), nothing will change in your future financial situation.

As a result, you may create stress about your current or future situation.

Effort encourages success and success fuels effort. Practice the new skills you have learned until they become second nature to you, just like driving a car, brushing your teeth, and getting dressed.

The learning cycle

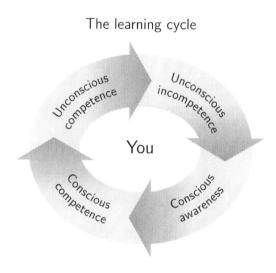

Figure 10.1: The learning cycle

Because human beings are learning machines, to grow as people we seek more learning. Keep in mind what I call "the learning cycle" (figure 10.1). We begin with unconscious incompetence, where you don't know that you don't know something. For example, at age one you didn't know that you didn't know how to cook. At some stage, you realised that you did not know something—you became consciously aware of your incompetence. Perhaps you were home alone as a teenager one day, you were hungry, and you realised you did not know how to cook. So you decided to learn from mum or dad, or by taking cooking lessons. With some practice, you learned how to cook some meals and you became consciously competent, aware that you knew how to cook. With more practice cooking those same meals, you refined your skill and you learned how to cook those meals without a recipe. You were on autopilot and you reached unconscious competence, where you did not know that you were doing it. It was effortless for you. Then, to keep growing as people, we continue to repeat the learning cycle for other skills.

It is the same with the skills and techniques that you have learned in this book. Before you read this book, there were some things you didn't know you didn't know—perhaps as you were reading this book you even thought to yourself, "I didn't know that." You were at **unconscious incompetence**. Then, as you started reading this book, you realised that there were some things that you needed to learn—you became **consciously aware** of that. You also moved into **conscious competence** by consciously practising these techniques and skills. Now, with extra practice, you will become **unconsciously competent**, and you will be using these techniques and skills without even being aware of them. Then you will have reached excellence with that skill and will move on to learn the next one. Until then—time to put on your "P" (practice) plates!

10.1   Design your own practice plan

It is now time to put your insights and learnings into action! To help you with practising and designing your own practice plan, I have suggested at the end of each chapter in this book that you write down your action journey steps along the way, and put them all in the one place for easy reference—in this chapter. If you have been doing this along the way, your own practice plan is almost ready. If not, you may like to go back and review your key learnings from each chapter and record these below now.

Step 1—Your learnings

Please write below your learnings from each chapter. Notice next to each learning what you want to practice to implement it in your own life and empower yourself for greater confidence and success.

Chapter 1

My learnings	What I want to practise
e.g. when I stop making excuses I will have more confidence and success	e.g. to take responsibility for my thoughts, feelings, and actions, and for changing any sabotaging ones

Chapter 2

My learnings	What I want to practise

Chapter 3

My learnings	What I want to practise

Chapter 4

My learnings	What I want to practise

Chapter 5

My learnings	What I want to practise

Chapter 6

My learnings	What I want to practise

Chapter 7

My learnings	What I want to practise

Chapter 8

My learnings	What I want to practise

Chapter 9

My learnings	What I want to practise

Chapter 10

You can add your learnings from this chapter once you finish reading it.

My learnings	What I want to practise

Step 2—Your priorities and action

By now you will have worked through many exercises in this book. You may or may not be feeling overwhelmed by the number of learnings and things you wish to practice to have the ongoing confidence and success you desire. For some people, it may all seem too much, and because they feel overwhelmed by this, they give up, as it seems too hard. I want you to know that it can be easier than you think.

The first step is to stop feeling overwhelmed, as that will prevent you from taking any action. Overwhelm occurs when you focus on too many things at once, or think about how much you need to do. Often people who feel overwhelmed place the same importance on everything, so little or nothing gets done. Instead, learn to prioritise.

Read through the above learnings and prioritise the things you want to practice below. Ask yourself, "What is the most important thing I want to do right now?" Then repeat this question until you have prioritised all the things you want to practice. Next to each priority, write down how often you would like to practice it (e.g. daily, weekly) and the date you will begin to practice it.

Priority	Practice	How often	Begin
1			
2			
3			

Priority	Practice	How often	Begin

Be realistic with your timeframes to set yourself up for success, as discussed in the goal-setting section of Chapter 7. One by one, take the actions by the date on your plan. Only focus on the action you are taking and enjoy the journey. To avoid overwhelm, only focus on the next action once the previous one is completed.

If you find yourself overwhelmed by a specific task, here are some questions you can ask yourself to get clarity and get started on taking action:

- What, specifically, do I want to do to complete this task?
- Who, specifically, do I want to talk to or get help from to complete this task?
- How, specifically, can I complete this task—what are the steps or processes?

As you take action, avoid getting bogged down by a task. Being bogged down in the detail of a task can make it difficult for you to see the forest from the trees, can have you go off-track, not be as productive as you could be, and have you not complete the task as a result. To stop being bogged down in the detail and empower yourself, here are some questions you can ask yourself:

- What is my intention for completing this task?
- What is my objective for this task?
- What is my outcome for completing this task?

Once you are clear about your outcome and what that task will help you achieve, you will find the clarity and motivation to take action towards completing it.

Step 3—Your weekly review

At the end of each week, set aside ten to fifteen minutes to review your progress on the above. Coach yourself for success by asking yourself three questions:

- What did I do well this week?

- What could I have improved?
- Overall, how well did I do?

For example:

> What I did well this week: I took action on my first two priorities that I committed to doing this week. I feel really happy with myself and notice a big improvement in my confidence. One area I could improve is to practice the skills first thing in the morning so that I do them daily, rather than when I remember to do them. Overall, I am excited about my progress this week.

Your answers to the above three questions become your feedback for success, helping you learn and grow from your actions. Rather than only focusing on what you could improve, importantly, these questions help you acknowledge successes on your journey to the next level of your personal and professional performance.

You can make a note of your weekly feedback below or in a separate journal.

My feedback this week

What did I do well this week?

_____

_____

_____

_____

What could I have improved?

_____

_____

Overall, how well did I do?

_____

Step 4—Refine your plan

Incorporate the above feedback to adjust your plan each week, until it works smoothly for you. Remember to play to your strengths. If you are more alert in the mornings, use that time for actions that benefit from your alertness. If you are most creative at night, do creative things then. If you are tired in the evenings, do routine tasks that require little energy—where you go into autopilot and you just do them.

You can make a note of any refinements to your plan below.

_____

_____

_____

_____

_____

_____

Step 5—Put off procrastination

In the absence of action, your unconscious can also remind you that you need to do something; it may bring up other issues for you to address because you have not taken the required action. It is one way your unconscious is getting you to pay attention and to do something different. If you ignore the early warning signs, your unconscious will give you bigger signs that are harder for you to ignore. Make sure you take the action you commit to doing.

Some people have mastered the art of putting off doing certain tasks, despite knowing that they will be worse off for the delay. Research has shown that around 15% to 20% of adults regularly put off activities that would be better done right away. Around 40% of people have experienced a financial loss as a result of procrastination, and procrastinators have higher stress levels and more severe health problems than people who act right away.

Should you contemplate putting off an activity from now on, below are three simple techniques to assist you with getting motivated and taking action.

1. Is it what you really want?

Think about the activity you are about to put off and ask yourself: "Is the activity aligned with my life purpose and goals? Will it bring me closer to my purpose and goals or steer me in another direction?"

By asking yourself these questions, you may find that the activity is not going to help you achieve what you want and you have been considering putting it off for the right reason. It is important to then act on that insight.

If the activity is aligned with your purpose and goals, perhaps you needed to see the fit with the big picture before you were motivated enough to do it. When we do things without a big-picture context, we can feel unmotivated, or see no real reason or benefit for doing it. Without a clear big picture to give us direction, we can more easily be distracted and procrastinate.

Once you are clear about the big picture, then ensure that you have clear goals with clear commitments and timeframes to help you to achieve your purpose and vision. Ensure that your goals are SMART, as we discussed in Chapter 7.

People with vague goals are almost as unmotivated as those without any goals at all! Research at Hofstra University demonstrates that procrastinators who had clear intentions and specific commitments to a time were eight times more likely to follow through on the commitment than those without them.

2. Are you sufficiently motivated?

As you think about the activity that you have been considering putting off, how motivated do you feel about doing it? As discussed in Chapter 3, motivation is a feeling, so do you actually feel motivated as you think about the activity or not? Do you feel other positive emotions like confidence, passion, and determination, or negative emotions such as resentment, guilt, shame, or anger, as you think about doing it?

It is difficult to put off doing things that you feel motivated to do. To get into a motivated frame of mind, use your motivation or resource anchor (Chapter 5). Once you are in the motivated frame of mind, you will find it easier to get started on any activity.

3. What meaning do you give it?

What meaning do you give to the activity that you have been considering putting off? Do you imagine it as being boring or fun? Do you imagine that it will take forever or be quick? Do you imagine that you will be able to do it easily, or worry that you will stumble or get stuck? If you imagine positives around that activity, you will be more motivated than if you imagine the negatives.

For some procrastinators, anticipation of the task is often far worse than how the task turns out. Are you anticipating the task turning out well or not? By visualising the activity being a success (as discussed in Chapter 5), you will be much more motivated to take action.

Imagine how much more productive, confident, and successful you will be once you master motivation and put off procrastination!

Step 6—Acknowledge yourself

Our confidence largely depends on the relationship we have with ourselves. As discussed earlier in this book, if we beat up on ourselves and have a lot of negative self-talk, this will reduce our level of confidence. In contrast, when we appreciate ourselves and acknowledge our achievements, this helps enormously in boosting our confidence.

Begin to acknowledge yourself right now, by thinking about your day and what you have accomplished, however small or large. You can make a note of your daily successes, achievements, and wins below or in a separate journal.

_____

_____

_____

_____

_____

_____

_____

_____

Step 7—Embrace challenges

The more confidence you have, the more committed you will be to yourself and your goals in life. In the face of challenges, your confidence and self-belief will help you conquer any challenges with determination. When faced with obstacles, rather than giving up you will see these as opportunities to show your commitment to yourself and your goals.

Remember that challenges can occur at any time in life. For example, after weeding your garden, you will need to maintain the garden and keep weeding it to have a weed-free garden. How will you deal with the "weeds" in your life from now on, so that you have the confidence and success you want in your life? Will you:

- go into denial and see the "weeds," yet say "there are no weeds," while the challenges remain unaddressed and things in your life remain unchanged; or

- wallow in the "weeds" and feel bad, losing confidence and negatively affecting your success? or
- acknowledge the "weeds" and deal with them effectively, using the techniques you have learned in this book to strengthen your confidence and success.

How you deal with challenges in your life is the key! It is your choice. With the techniques you have learned in this book, you now have some effective resources to embrace and deal with life's challenges, and to stop sabotaging your confidence and success. You also now have your own personal practice plan that, when consistently implemented, will help you to empower yourself for greater confidence and success.

10.2   Summary

The key messages that we covered in this chapter include:

- Action creates momentum; create your own luck by taking action and making things happen.
- You can easily put your insights and learnings from reading this book into practice by designing and following your own practice plan.
- Make sure you prioritise the things you choose to practice and that you set yourself up for success with realistic timeframes.
- Because confidence largely depends on the relationship you have with yourself, it is important to acknowledge yourself each day for your accomplishments and successes.
- How you deal with challenges in your life is the key! You

now have the techniques to embrace and deal with life's challenges more effectively, as well as the techniques to empower yourself for greater confidence and success.

Enjoy the journey, remember to celebrate your successes, and keep being the magnificent person you know you are ... inside.

Appendix

In this appendix, you will find additional resources to empower you.

Your questions and successes

I welcome any questions, insights, and successes that you have from completing the exercises in this book. Please feel free to email me directly at vesna@qttransformation.com. I look forward to hearing from you and personally replying to you.

Free resources

If you would like additional resources to assist you on your journey of empowerment, please visit our website to receive your FREE gifts: www.qttransformation.com.

Additional transformational resources

Throughout this book, we have made reference to addressing all negative emotions associated with all past events, all limiting beliefs, and deep-seated internal conflicts. If you would like to address these so that you too can transform your confidence and success in a fast and lasting way with the help of a fully trained and certified NLP/Hypnotherapy Master Practitioner/Trainer, please email me at vesna@qttransformation.com and I or one of our fully qualified Q^t licensees will be delighted to assist you.

If you would like additional information about our Q^t transformational personalised consultations, seminars or certification trainings, please visit www.qttransformation.com.

If you are interested in learning more about NLP and Hypnotherapy and how you can help others to transform their lives, please email me at vesna@qttransformation.com for details of our upcoming certification trainings and Q^t licensee opportunities.

In addition to communication, how we relate to other people's behaviour is very important. This is a huge topic in itself, which I thoroughly researched as part of my PhD thesis. In the process, I discovered a new filter (Q^t respect^i) and behavioural change techniques to assist us with effectively dealing with people and their behaviour. You can personally experience these in Q^t's exclusive programs. Simply email me at vesna@qttransformation.com for details.

Upcoming books

Another area that I am also passionate about is the mind–body connection. If you are interested in learning more about how the mind-body works and how you can reprogram it for optimal health, I discuss this in detail in a chapter I contributed to in an upcoming book.

If you enjoyed reading and experiencing the techniques in this book, look out for the upcoming sequel to this book. I will assist you to explore and gain an even deeper perspective on yourself. You will learn even more powerful techniques to assist you to transform your personal and professional success.

Please email me at vesna@qttransformation.com for more details of these upcoming books.

Q^t 7 Secrets to Transformation®, *Q^t Transform Your Destiny*®, *Q^t Performance Transformation Expert*®, Q^t, Q^t respect^i and respect^i are all registered trademarks of Vesna Corporation Pty Ltd. *Q^t 7 Secrets to Transformation*® and *Q^t Transform Your Destiny*® seminar licenses are issued by Dr Vesna Grubacevic and Vesna Corporation Pty Ltd.

Acknowledgements

Writing, publishing, and marketing this book has been and continues to be a team effort. I sincerely thank all the wonderful members of my team, from the amazingly talented colleagues, editors, proofreaders, publishing team, marketing and publicity support—you are all treasured and valued. Thank you!

There are so many people I would like to thank. Rather than listing the numerous team members involved in this exciting project, and risking missing out on anyone, I thank you again individually and collectively.

You are my Star Team! Anything and everything is possible with your attitude and competence. You walk your talk when it comes to confidence and success, and I am proud, honoured, and privileged to have you on my team. Thank you!

About the author

Dr **Vesna Grubacevic**, author of *Stop Sabotaging Your Confidence*, is a Performance Transformation Expert®, founder of the award-winning company Q^t, and an internationally recognised and Certified NLP & Hypnotherapy Trainer, Master Practitioner, and Clinical Hypnotherapist. She also holds a PhD and a Bachelor of Economics. Dr Vesna extensively contributes articles and media commentary, is a sought-after, passionate, and innovative speaker, and is the creator of breakthrough behavioural change techniques.

With well over thirty years of experience in business (including in economics, domestic and international financial markets, global strategy, cultural change in multinational organisations, and hospitality, and working with CEOs, executives, professionals, salespeople, business owners, managers, teams and individuals), Dr Vesna has mastered the art and science of understanding behaviour and performance on an individual, business, organisational, economy-wide, and global level.

Her diversity of experience with corporations, business, health, spirituality, and the arts enables Dr Vesna to understand, relate easily to, and be in tune with people from any field. This experience, combined with a sense of fun, passion, and an innate ability to simply, effectively, and clearly communicate the most complex of concepts makes her unique in her fields.

Having had many challenges with lack of confidence in her personal and professional life, Dr Vesna has been through her own personal transformation journey, growing from decades of being bullied to become a confident and successful business owner. She now inspires others to stop sabotaging their confidence and success and to realise their potential.

She founded Q^t in 2000, driven by her vision of creating an empowered society. Since then, she has run numerous NLP/Hypnotherapy certification trainings, and trained and certified many successful practitioners, including coaches, therapists, health practitioners, managers, business owners, and leaders to empower others.

Dr Vesna has also worked with thousands of individuals and professionals to transform their personal and professional success, as well as assisting businesses to transform their individual, team, and leadership performance and business culture. This book is aimed at reaching many more people and empowering the lives of readers and those around them.

Dr Vesna's passion for transformation and empowering others to excel personally and professionally is reflected in the exceptional results she achieves with her clients. Often described by her clients, colleagues, and friends as having the highest levels of integrity, professionalism, ethics, and congruence, Dr Vesna lives and breathes all that she teaches. Her drive for excellence and dedication to her clients is reflected in her proven track record of empowering clients to achieve exceptional personal and professional results, fast.